BLOG SOCIAL MEDIA:

BLOG	www.DessertsWithBenefits.com
FACEBOOK	www.facebook.com/DessertsWithBenefits
TWITTER	www.twitter.com/DWBenefits
PINTEREST	www.pinterest.com/WithBenefits
TUMBLR	www.DessertsWithBenefits.tumblr.com
INSTAGRAM	www.instagram.com/DessertsWithBenefits

Tweet me @DWBenefits and #DessertsWithBenefits!

Instagram me @DessertsWithBenefits and #DessertsWithBenefits!

Library of Congress Control Number: 2015916253
CreateSpace Independent Publishing Platform, North Charleston, SC

ISBN-13: 978-1511416580
ISBN-10: 1511416580

First Edition

French Macarons (pg. 64-67) with
Chocolate Frosting (pg. 155)

TABLE OF CONTENTS

Red Velvet Cake (pg. 94-95) with
White Chocolate Cream Cheese Frosting (pg. 152-153)

ABOUT THE AUTHOR

Jessica Stier is the author, photographer and recipe developer behind the *Naughty or Nice* cookbook, which was inspired by her healthy dessert recipe blog, Desserts with Benefits™ (www.DessertsWithBenefits.com).

Jessica is a healthy dessert expert with an interest and a strong scholarly background in the fields of Nutrition and Dietetics (thanks, university!), but before college she was the complete opposite…

I guess we should start from the beginning, shall we?

I was born and raised in a quiet, homey neighborhood in Calgary, Alberta, Canada. Like most kids, I ate whatever (and whenever) I pleased. I plowed my way through boxes of candy bars, jumbo-sized bags of chocolatey goodies, and enough candy to fill dozens of those Halloween trick-or-treat pumpkin baskets (aka, enough sugar to make even the most seasoned sugar fiend sick with a stomachache and candy hangover).

When my family and I moved to the United States, so did my sugar addiction. Up to the age of eighteen, I ate poorly (ehem, understatement of the year, ehem) and didn't exercise. At all. I ate chocolate bars for breakfast (yes, I'm serious), a bag of chips, "fruit" snacks, and a carton of sugary chocolate milk for lunch (are you getting a sugar rush just by reading this?), and something totally useless for dinner, like nachos or instant noodles. I brought so much candy to school that I was known as "Hershey Girl," "Sourpatch Girl," and even just the plain old, "girl with candy" (I went through a few candy phases). I needed $20 per week to support my daily vending machine visits and another $20 on top of that to pay for my hefty lunches.

After every meal, I felt gross and nauseous with a foggy brain, but I kept on eating the unhealthy foods I had always eaten. I mean, a diet like that was normal to me. My family ate like that, the kids at school ate like that, it all tasted good… so, what's the problem?

Why change?

When I turned sixteen and got my first job at a pretzel joint in the local shopping mall, I gained a little bit of weight. And by "a little" I mean "a lot." Like, twelve pounds in three months. This was a huge shock to me. I never gained weight like that before despite my inadequate diet and sedentary lifestyle. I may have been on the thin side my entire life, but I was always "skinny-fat." A lot of jiggle on bones with no muscle whatsoever.

My solution? Oh, just buy those 100-calorie snack packs and (attempt to) stop eating a bajillion pretzels dunked in butter every time they began to look dry. Yeah, that didn't fly. The excess salt, the dangerous trans fats, the highly refined sugar, the artificial sweeteners… they just made me want more. A lot more. And I paid the price for it – I was an emotional roller coaster with crazy cravings, either trapped in a steady state of lethargy or stuck in an unstoppable yo-yoing between sugar rush and sugar crash.

I just wanted to be better… **healthier**.

With perfect timing, I graduated high school and was about to enter university – a brand new stage in life where I decided to start over. Completely. I chose to major in Nutritional Sciences, which turned out to be one of the best decisions I have ever made in my life. I learned everything under the sun about food, nutrition, and the human body. I finally came to terms with my own body, the reasons why I ate the way I did, and how I should be eating. Now, just a few years later, I have finally found the solution to achieving consistent energy levels, and I am satiated for a long period of time (no more of those "I-must-eat-that-entire-tray-of-brownies-ASAP" feelings). I have boosted my metabolism, I have put on lean muscle, and my body fat percentage has dropped.

~~I lived for chocolate.~~ I live for chocolate.

Don't get me wrong, I still indulge. I have (and will always have) a serious passion for sweets! I have just learned how to make those sweets (secretly) healthy.

Enter, **Desserts with Benefits**™

My blog was born late at night on April 20th, 2011 as a serious procrastination technique to avoid studying for finals. I didn't post a recipe, but rather, a list of desserts that were on my "Recipe Wishlist," along with dishes that I've made but had turned out unsuccessful. Healthy baking is a difficult thing to do! I don't use refined sugar (white granulated sugar, brown sugar, high-fructose corn syrup, etc.), artificial sweeteners (aspartame, sucralose, etc.), white flour (all purpose flour, cake flour, pastry flour, bread flour, bleached flours, etc.), or unhealthy fats (hydrogenated oil, shortening, margarine, etc.). I mean, anything can be made to taste good using all the wrong ingredients, but is it what your body wants? I don't want my desserts to give off the same repercussions that typical unhealthy desserts do (aka, bloating, headache, stomachache, nausea).

When I started blogging, I hoped to show people that healthy ingredients *can* indeed make a delicious cake, muffin, pastry, cookie, and so on.

I am happy to say that, with the hundreds of testimonials I've received, with the loyal Desserts with Benefits™ fans who comment regularly, and with the thousands upon thousands of people around the world who have tried (and loved!) my recipes…

I have met that goal.

ABOUT THE COOKBOOK

Naughty or Nice is a collection of 70 homemade treats that taste like sinfully decadent, naughty desserts… it just so happens that they're secretly healthy, and thus, nice! *Naughty or Nice* makes it possible to eat healthy and stay sane. It's a sinless love affair between decadent desserts and healthy eats.

So *indulge*… no strings attached!

One bite of the Fudge Brownies (pg. 76-77) or a forkful of the Classic Cheesecake (pg. 122-123) and you'll be screaming, "OH MY GOSH this is so freakin' good how can this be good for me?!?" If you were served two scoops of Vanilla Bean Ice Cream – one from this cookbook (pg. 140-141) and one from the grocery store – I'm *preeeetty* darn sure you'll be stumped on which one is the healthy version.

This cookbook has options for everyone: gluten-free, dairy-free, nut-free, soy-free, eggless, vegan… even sugar-free, refined sugar-free, cholesterol-free, low-calorie, low-sodium, high-fiber and high-protein. These recipes might be "free" of some stuff, but they sure aren't free of flavor!

Every recipe in this cookbook is all natural – no artificial sweeteners, no synthetic food dyes, no artificial food flavorings, no hydrogenated oils, and no preservatives whatsoever. That list right there is unheard of when it comes to store-bought desserts.

These recipes are a total godsend for the health conscious dessert lovers out there (aka, YOU). If you occasionally crave (and when I say "occasionally," I really mean "constantly") a big hunk of – for lack of a better word – sugar in a wrapper, make a batch of DIY candies (pg. 40-45) instead and you'll be happy as can be… no guilt involved.

Each recipe in this cookbook includes a nutrition label so you can see how many calories, grams of fat, carbohydrates, protein, fiber, etc. are in each serving. The recipes in this cookbook are nutritionally balanced with healthy fats, complex carbohydrates, slow-digesting fiber and satiating protein. I like to have my recipes fall somewhere within these ranges, but we don't need to go all "Anal Retentive Chef" here (thanks, SNL!):

20-35% of calorie intake from fat
45-65% of calorie intake from carbohydrates
10-35% of calorie intake from protein

These recommended percentages have a pretty wide range, and depending on what stage you are in your life – whether you're an athlete or a vegan, whether you're a growing teen or a pregnant woman, etc. – you can modify these numbers to suit your body's needs. I always recommend meeting with a registered dietician if you need some help (they don't bite, I swear)!

Let's all skip the store-bought desserts and make our own right at home. And while we're at it, let's make it *good* for us.

After experiencing so much support and success with my first cookbook, *DIY Protein Bars*, I knew another cookbook would need to be underway!

DIY Protein Bars has a very focused theme – solely protein bars – while *Naughty or Nice* has a much broader range. It's got cakes, it's got cookies, it's got brownies... plus ice cream and cheesecakes and frostings and more.

If you want to check out my other cookbook, search "*DIY Protein Bars*" on Amazon.com:

I wouldn't have been able to write this cookbook without all the diehard Desserts with Benefits™ fans, and for that, I am beyond thankful.

With every comment, I am ecstatic.

With every email, I am touched.

With every shout-out, I am over the moon.

With every testimonial, I am eternally grateful.

With all the encouragement, my nerves poof into thin air.

The incredibly friendly and uplifting online community that I am in inspires me more than words can ever describe. So THANK YOU!

PANTRY STAPLES

NUTS AND NUT BUTTERS

Nuts are full of healthy fats, fiber and essential nutrients. While they are high in protein, they are incomplete proteins (they lack essential amino acids) so they need to be paired with something else to create a complete protein, such as oats, rice, beans, etc. Always use natural nut butters without added sugar, salt and oil – the ingredient list should contain only one ingredient: the nut itself! Slightly runny nut butters are ideal for these recipes. Try to buy organic and non-GMO. To save money, you can make nut butters at home (see pg. 32 and pg. 156 for instructions).

- Macadamia Nuts (raw or roasted)
- Pecans
- Hazelnuts (raw or roasted)

- Roasted Almond Butter
- Natural Roasted Peanut Butter
- Raw Coconut Butter

PROTEIN POWDERS

Brown Rice Protein Powder

Brown rice protein powder is hypoallergenic (gluten-free, dairy-free, nut-free) and vegan. I use SunWarrior® Classic Protein in Vanilla. I like this protein powder because it is non-GMO and sugar-free.

Brown rice protein powder cannot be omitted. It might be possible to substitute it with other vegan protein powders (such as hemp, pea or soy), but every brand is different so I can't vouch for them. All I know is that whey, casein, and egg white protein powders will not work in place of the brown rice protein powder.

Whey Protein Powder

Whey protein powder is widely available and is perfect for people who aren't vegan or allergic to dairy. I use Bodylogix® in both Vanilla and Chocolate because it is non-GMO, sugar-free, and sourced from grass-fed cows. Avoid brands that use artificial flavors, artificial sweeteners and food dyes.

FLOURS

Almond Meal

Almond meal is ground up *blanched* almonds (different from Almond Flour, which is ground up unblanched almonds, skins and all). I use Bob's Red Mill® almond meal.

Brown Rice Flour

Coconut Flour

Coconut flour has a mild, sweet coconut flavor. I use Coconut Secret® or Nutiva® because they are gluten-free, organic and non-GMO. Coconut flour cannot be replaced because it provides a unique texture and absorbs a lot of liquid.

Oat Flour

Oat flour is simply ground up oats. I use Bob's Red Mill® certified gluten-free oat flour because it's whole grain, finely ground, easy to use, safe for people with celiac disease, and has a great flavor. Oat flour is difficult to replace because it acts as a binder and absorbs quite a bit of liquid.

Peanut Flour

Peanut flour is a partially defatted flour made from ground peanuts. I use Protein Plus® roasted all-natural peanut flour, which is high-protein, reduced-fat and gluten-free. Peanut flour is difficult to replace because it acts as a binder, absorbs a lot of liquid, and provides extra peanut flavor.

¼ cup of **peanut flour** has 110 calories, 4g fat, 8g carbs, 4g fiber and 16g protein.
¼ cup of **peanuts** has 170 calories, 14g fat, 5g carbs, 2g fiber and 7g protein.

Quinoa Flour

Quinoa flour has a very strong flavor, so it takes some getting used to, but it's healthy and a complete protein! I use Ancient Harvest® quinoa flour.

Organic Soy Flour

Soy flour is made from ground soybeans. *Always* use organic soy flour to avoid pesticides, additives and genetically modified ingredients. I use Bob's Red Mill® organic soy flour, which is whole grain, high-protein, high-fiber, low-carb, and high in minerals. Soy flour is difficult to replace because it provides a unique texture and absorbs a lot of liquid.

Sweet White Sorghum Flour

Sorghum flour works best when combined with other flours. Alone, it tends to yield a baked good with a crumbly texture. I use Bob's Red Mill® sorghum flour.

CHOCOLATE

No-Sugar-Added Milk Chocolate (I use Lily's® or Coco Polo®)

No-Sugar-Added Dark Chocolate (70% cacao, I use Coco Polo®)

No-Sugar-Added Dark Chocolate Baking Chips (I use Lily's®)

Unsweetened Natural Cocoa Powder

Unsweetened Dutch Processed Cocoa Powder

Organic Raw Cacao Butter (Food Grade)

SWEETENERS

Liquid Stevia Extract

Stevia is an all-natural, calorie-free, sugar-free sweetener (derived from the Stevia rebaudiana herb) that does not affect blood glucose levels. It's 300x sweeter than sugar, so it's really easy to use too much, causing the dish you're making to taste bitter. I use SweetLeaf® Stevia Clear (Plain) because it tastes great and it's organic. Always use alcohol-free stevia.

Pure Maple Syrup

Molasses (Unsulphured)

I consider molasses to be more of a "flavoring" rather than a sweetener. It has a very strong flavor and a very thick texture. It's low-glycemic and high in vitamins and minerals. I use Wholesome Sweeteners® unsulphured molasses.

Erythritol (Powdered and Granulated)

Erythritol (pronounced: ear-eeth-rit-all) sounds like a chemical, but rest assured, it is an *all-natural*, sugar-free sweetener. We shouldn't judge it by its name or because we may have trouble pronouncing it… after all, we can pronounce "trans fats" and "Red Dye #40" but those things sure aren't good for us! I use Now Foods® granulated erythritol and Swerve® powdered (confectioners) erythritol (both are non-GMO).
¼ cup of **erythritol** has 12 calories, 3g carbs and 0g sugar.
¼ cup of **sugar** has 192 calories, 48g carbs and 48g sugar.

Evaporated Cane Juice

Evaporated Cane Juice is like a mix between sucanat and white sugar – it isn't brown and chunky like sucanat, and it isn't highly refined or bleached like white sugar… it's *juuuust* right. I use Wholesome Sweeteners® evaporated cane juice because it's organic, non-GMO and fair trade.

Sucanat

Sucanat is an unrefined sugar that contains the natural molasses from the sugar cane. It's chunky, has a dark tan color, and tastes like brown sugar. I use Wholesome Sweeteners® sucanat.

FLAVORINGS

Always use natural flavors. If available, use organic too!

Natural Flavors

- Almond Extract (I use Simply Organic®)
- Butter Flavor (I use LorAnn Oils® or Silver Cloud Estates®… whichever is cheapest)

    Note: LorAnn Oils® sells a similar flavoring – Butter-Vanilla Bakery Emulsion – but it contains hydrogenated oils!
    Only buy the Butter Bakery Emulsion, which is all-natural, trans fat-free, sugar-free, gluten-free and vegan.

- Coconut Flavor (I use Bakto Flavors®… make sure to use *natural flavor* and not imitation flavor)
- Mint Flavor (I use Frontier Co-Op®)
- Peppermint Flavor (I use Simply Organic®)
- Strawberry Flavor (I use Bakto Flavors®)
- Vanilla Bean Pods
- Vanilla Extract (I use homemade [see Note] or Nielsen Massey®)
- Vanilla Bean Paste (I use homemade [see Note] or Nielsen Massey®)

    Note: You can make Vanilla Extract and Vanilla Bean Paste at home! Just go to www.DessertsWithBenefits.com
    and in the search bar, type in: "Homemade Vanilla Extract"
    or "Homemade Vanilla Bean Paste"

Spices and Strong Flavors

- Ground Cinnamon, Ginger and Nutmeg
- Salt (sometimes I use Pink Himalayan Salt)
- Instant Coffee Granules (you can use decaf if you want)
- Brewed Espresso (you can use decaf if you want)
- Matcha Green Tea Powder (I use DoMatcha®)

Add-Ins

- Poppyseeds
- Natural Food Coloring (I use Natures Flavors®/Seelect Tea® rainbow pack, which comes with red ["Cherry Red"], orange ["Pumpkin Orange"], yellow, green ["Forest Green"] and blue)

Key Baking Ingredients

- Baking Soda
- Double-Acting Baking Powder
- Xanthan Gum (I use Bob's Red Mill®)
- White Vinegar
- Cooking Spray (I use my Misto® Sprayer filled with Grapeseed Oil)

OTHER ESSENTIALS

Active Dry Yeast

Arrowroot Starch
Other starches may be substituted, however, some are stronger/weaker than arrowroot and may alter the recipe's final outcome.

Black Beans and Garbanzo Beans/Chickpeas
I use canned black beans and chickpeas. Use unsalted if you can find it!

Crispy Brown Rice Cereal
I use Erewhon® because it's organic, gluten-free and whole-grain.

Coconut Oil
Unrefined coconut oil has a strong coconut flavor while refined coconut oil is neutral. Choose whichever kind you want, just make sure it's non-hydrogenated!

Reduced Fat Unsweetened Shredded Coconut
I use Let's Do…Organic® shredded coconut because it's organic and contains no added sugar.

Organic Low Fat Cottage Cheese

Organic Neufchâtel Cream Cheese
If you can't find Neufchâtel, just use ⅓ Less Fat Cream Cheese (they're basically the same thing).

Ground Flaxseed
I use Bob's Red Mill® organic whole ground flaxseed meal.

100% Fruit Spread (no sugar added)
I use St. Dalfour® or Nature's Hollow® in strawberry, but you can use whatever flavor you want.

Unflavored Gelatin

Plain, Nonfat Greek Yogurt
Always buy plain, unsweetened yogurt to avoid the added sugar, food dyes and other additives. Get organic to avoid the added hormones, antibiotics, steroids, etc.

Organic Dried Nonfat Milk

Old Fashioned Rolled Oats and Quick Cooking Oats
I use Bob's Red Mill® certified gluten-free old fashioned rolled oats and quick cooking oats.

100% Organic Orange Juice

Psyllium Husk Powder
I use Now Foods® psyllium husk powder. Be sure to use the powder and not the whole psyllium husks.

Organic Cage-Free Eggs

Organic Extra Firm Tofu

FRUITS AND VEGETABLES

Fruits and vegetables provide natural sweetness along with some fiber, vitamins and minerals. Always seek organic, non-GMO fruits and veggies with no added sugar.

Fresh and Frozen

- Bananas
- Beets
- Blueberries
- Carrots
- Lemons
- Baby Spinach
- Strawberries

Dried

- Unsweetened Raisins

Freeze-Dried

- Freeze-Dried Strawberries

Packaged and Canned

- Unsweetened Applesauce
- Canned 100% Pure Pumpkin Purée

MILK AND NON-DAIRY MILKS

Organic Half and Half

When purchasing dairy products, always buy organic and grass-fed when available. As a college student, I took a course on cows and dairy farming taught by a former member of Monsanto®. It suffices to say that conventional dairy farming practices are deplorable to me, and I sure don't want to support the corporations that employ them.

Unsweetened Vanilla Almond Milk

I use Silk® unsweetened vanilla almond milk (30 calories per cup). Unsweetened Vanilla Soy, Coconut, Cashew, Hemp and Rice Milk should work just fine too! If using soymilk, always buy organic and non-GMO, never conventional.

Canned Light Coconut Milk

When recipes in this cookbook call for coconut milk, it is always canned coconut milk, not cartoned.

ESSENTIAL KITCHEN TOOLS

MAJOR APPLIANCES: Fridge, Freezer, Microwave, Stove and Oven

Kitchen Weigh Scale (a must must must!)

I make every single recipe using a kitchen scale. In my kitchen, a scale is more important than measuring cups. In this books' recipes, I start off each ingredient by weight, and then in parentheses, the estimated equivalent in volume. Weighing your ingredients is much more accurate than measuring ingredients with measuring cups. 1 cup of Oat Flour will weigh about 120g sifted, or 180g packed… that is a huge difference that will lead to an even bigger difference in taste, texture and appearance. So stick with the scale!

I use my Escali® Arti Glass Kitchen Scale.

Electric Stand Mixer with Beater and Whisk Attachments

Many recipes in this cookbook use an electric stand mixer. It mixes batters and doughs thoroughly, quickly and easily. Sometimes you can do without the stand mixer and mix everything by hand, just know that it will take longer and require a bit more patience!

I use my KitchenAid® Artisan® Series 5-Quart Tilt-Head Stand Mixer.

Ice Cream Maker

I use my KitchenAid® Ice Cream Maker Attachment (makes up to 2 Quarts)

Food Processor

I use my Hamilton Beach® 10-Cup Food Processor with Compact Storage.

High-Speed Blender

I use my NutriBullet® Pro 900.

Mixing Bowls

Have small-, medium- and large-sized bowls. Make sure they're microwave-safe too.

Measuring Spoons

Have ⅛ tsp, ¼ tsp, ½ tsp, ¾ tsp, 1 tsp and 1 tbs.

Measuring Cups

Have ¼ cup, ⅓ cup, ½ cup and 1 cup.

Spoons, Forks, a Sharp 10" Knife, Kitchen Shears and Toothpicks

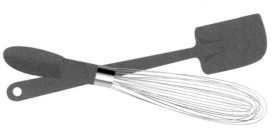

Wire Whisks and Silicone Spatulas

 2 12-cup Standard Cupcake Pans

 8x5" and 9x5x3" Loaf Pans

 2 8" Cake Pans and a 9" Springform Pan

8x8" Square Brownie Pan

13x18" Jelly Roll Pan

3 14x16" Flat Cookie Sheets

6 6oz Ramekins

2 Wire Cooling Racks

Fine Mesh Sieve

Rolling Pin

1¾" and 2" Circle Cookie Cutters

Pie Server

Microplane and Grater
To zest lemons and to grate carrots.

Medium Cookie Scoop (1¾" diameter)

Cake Pedestal and Cake Dome
You'll need this to frost and store cakes.

Plastic Wrap and Foil

Disposable Piping Bags with Closed Star Tip (#846), Round Tip (#804), and Small Round Tip (#4)

Candy Thermometer
    Candy thermometers are required in the recipes that call for them. A few degrees difference can determine whether or not the recipe is a success or a failure. For example, in the Homemade Chewy Caramels (pg. 44-45), too low of a temperature and you'll get syrup, too high of a temperature and you'll get brittle.

1.5-Quart and 3-Quart Saucepans

Double Boiler
    I use my Farberware® 2-Quart Covered Double Boiler. It's perfect for melting chocolate, caramels, cocoa butter, coconut oil and more.

Kitchen Blowtorch **(HELL YEEAAHHH!)**

Pre-Cut Parchment Baking Sheets (12½x16")
    I use If You Care® compostable, unbleached, chlorine-free parchment baking paper.

Parchment Paper Liners for 8" Cake Pans
    Essentially, this is pre-cut parchment paper in the shape of a circle to fit inside your cake pan and prevent sticking.

3 11⅝x16½" Silicone Baking Mats (I use Silpat®)

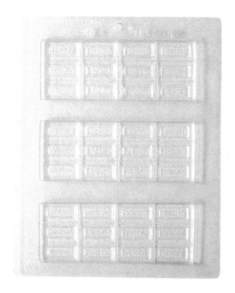

3 Chocolate Bar Molds

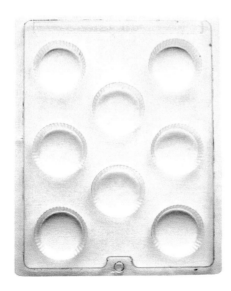

Peanut Butter Cup Mold

GETTING STARTED

HOW TO MELT CHOCOLATE

① Fill the bottom portion of a double boiler with 2-3" of water. Make sure the water doesn't touch the bottom of the double boiler insert! Place over a stove set to medium heat.

② While the water is heating up, break the chocolate into chunks and place inside the double boiler insert. When the water starts to simmer, reduce the heat to medium-low.

③ Stir occasionally until the chocolate is melted and completely smooth.

HOW TO LINE YOUR PAN WITH PARCHMENT PAPER

① Cut your parchment paper so that it fits nicely inside your pan. In this example, we are lining an 8x8" brownie pan. You'll need to cut the parchment paper into long strips that are slightly thinner than the size of the pan, about 7½" (if you are using the same pre-cut sheets that I use – If You Care® unbleached parchment baking paper – simply fold the paper in half and cut 1" off the creased side).

② Place the paper inside the pan, leaving the overhang for easy removal later on. Feel free to use mini binder clips on the sides of the pan to keep the paper in place. This makes it easier to spread and flatten thick doughs or batters inside the pan.

MONEY-SAVING TIPS

Tip #1: Shop around for the best prices. Find some coupons. Use a discount code!

I buy about 75% of my groceries and appliances online because, the majority of the time, they're far cheaper than store-bought goods. Grocery stores have to mark up their prices due to overhead costs, employees, waste, etc.

My favorite grocery stores include Whole Foods Market®, Costco®, Target®, H-E-B®, Safeway® and Trader Joe's®.

My favorite websites include Amazon.com, ThriveMarket.com, Netrition.com and iHerb.com.

Tip #2: Buy in bulk!

Food ingredients are most often cheaper in packs of 2, 3, 4, or more.

Tip #3: Make your nut butters at home!

Just go to www.DessertsWithBenefits.com and in the search bar, type in: "Raw Pecan Butter"

The process of making your own nut (or seed) butter is really the same for all nuts and seeds. Just swap the pecans in the original recipe with whatever nut/seed you like.

FINALLY ABOUT TO MAKE A RECIPE? CONGRATULATIONS! BUT, BEFORE YOU DO, READ THIS:

FIRST, just as a precaution, always read through the recipe once or twice from start to finish before diving in! Baking on the fly can lead to some serious kitchen fails. Trust me, I've come across every problem imaginable by cooking without reading the instructions first – *rolls eyes* – but I've learned my lesson. Avoid substituting and/or omitting ingredients because 99% of the time, the recipe will not work. And you will be sad. So sad. The recipes here are tried and true so we can love them just the way they are.

SECOND, you may notice that I use almond milk in the majority of the recipes. This is just my personal preference, as I love the flavor that Unsweetened Vanilla Almond Milk provides. If you don't want to use almond milk, you can try substituting it with your favorite milk or non-dairy milk. Just note that the nutrition label will change slightly, and the final product may have a different texture, flavor, and appearance.

THIRD, use a kitchen scale! In the Essential Kitchen Tools section (pg. 18), I mention how I use a kitchen scale to make all of my recipes. A scale allows you to measure ingredients correctly so that you get the same final product every time you make a recipe. However, accuracy isn't a scale's only purpose. Using a scale also allows you to make accurate nutrition labels (or simply calculate the correct number of calories, fat, carbs, protein, etc.). You also use less cooking materials – from mixing bowls to utensils to measuring cups to measuring spoons. Less dishes to wash? Yes, please. Because that gives us more time to eat… hehehe.

FOURTH, check your altitude! The altitude at which you bake affects a baked good's texture, density and moisture level, as well as how much it rises. All of the recipes in this cookbook were tested at sea level. If you live at a high altitude, check out this website before baking to find out what recipe adjustments need to be made:
www.epicurious.com/archive/howtocook/primers/altitudebaking_science

FIFTH, use an oven thermometer! Ovens are notorious for being slightly off kilter, so when baking, always use an oven thermometer to ensure it is at the correct temperature. A worthy mention here is that all of the recipes in this cookbook were tested with the oven rack placed in the center of the oven (unless otherwise noted in the recipe, such as the Lemon Bars [pg. 82-83] and Pumpkin Pie [pg. 134-135]).

If you have any other questions, feel free to ask me on my blog: www.DessertsWithBenefits.com
Okay, that's it. Now go make some healthy desserts! *fist pump*

Snacks & Treats

Homemade Chewy Caramels (pg. 44-45)

PEANUT BUTTER FUDGE

YIELD: **36 FUDGE CUBES**

440g (2 cups)	Organic Low Fat Cottage Cheese
1 teaspoon	Vanilla Extract
1 teaspoon	Natural Butter Flavor
158g (1 cup + 2 tablespoons)	Powdered Erythritol
150g (1¼ cups)	Peanut Flour
20g (2 tablespoons)	Psyllium Husk Powder

① Line an 8x8" brownie pan with parchment paper.

② In a food processor, add the cottage cheese, vanilla extract, butter flavor and erythritol. Purée until smooth. Pour the blended mixture (scrape out as much as you can!) into a stand mixer fitted with a beater attachment.

③ In a small bowl, stir together the peanut flour and psyllium. Dump the dry ingredients into the stand mixer and mix on low speed until the ingredients are fully incorporated. Scrape down the sides of the bowl. Mixture should be very thick and fudgy.

④ Scoop the mixture into the prepared pan and spread it out. Cover the pan with plastic wrap and refrigerate overnight.

⑤ The next day, slice the fudge into 36 cubes. Serve immediately, or store in a tightly sealed container in the fridge for up to 5 days.

Nutrition Facts

Serving Size Peanut Butter Fudge, 3 fudge cubes (65g)

Amount Per Serving

Calories 80	Calories from Fat 20

	%Daily Value*
Total Fat 2.5g	4%
Saturated Fat 0.5g	4%
Trans Fat 0g	
Cholesterol 5mg	2%
Sodium 150mg	6%
Total Carbohydrate 7g	2%
Dietary Fiber 3g	11%
Sugars 2g	
Protein 11g	

Vitamin A 0%	•	Vitamin C 0%
Calcium 4%	•	Iron 2%

CHOCOLATE-COVERED PEANUT BUTTER VARIATION:
MELT 4OZ OF YOUR FAVORITE CHOCOLATE. AFTER SLICING THE FUDGE INTO CUBES, COAT THE FUDGE WITH THE CHOCOLATE, REFRIGERATE TO FIRM, THEN SERVE!

HOMEMADE WHITE CHOCOLATE

YIELD: **8 BARS**

128g (½ cup)	Macadamia Butter
112g (½ cup)	Organic Raw Cacao Butter
140g (1 cup)	Powdered Erythritol
20g (2 tablespoons, packed)	Organic Dried Nonfat Milk
small pinch	Salt
½	Vanilla Bean Pod
½ teaspoon	Liquid Stevia Extract

FOR THE MACADAMIA BUTTER

① Add ~1½ cups of macadamia nuts (I used raw, but you can use roasted if you like) to a food processor. Pulse it a few times until the nuts turn into crumbles.

② Process for ~5 minutes straight, or until completely smooth. Scrape down the sides of the food processor when necessary.

FOR THE WHITE CHOCOLATE

③ Fill the bottom portion of a double boiler with 2-3" of water. Make sure the water doesn't touch the bottom of the double boiler insert! Place over a stove set to medium heat.

④ While the water heats up, add the macadamia butter and cacao butter into the double boiler insert. When the water starts to simmer, reduce the heat to medium-low. Whisk occasionally until completely melted. Turn the stove off.

⑤ In a small bowl, whisk together the erythritol, dried milk and salt. Slowly whisk into the stovetop mixture.

⑥ Split the vanilla bean pod and scrape out the seeds. Whisk the vanilla bean seeds into the stovetop mixture.

⑦ Whisk in the stevia extract (it will thicken). Spoon the mixture into 8 cavities of 3 chocolate bar molds (see Essential Kitchen Tools pg. 23). Refrigerate until firm. Store in a tightly sealed container in the fridge for up to 2 weeks.

Nutrition Facts	
Serving Size Homemade White Chocolate, 1 bar (50g)	
Amount Per Serving	
Calories 250	Calories from Fat 230
	%Daily Value*
Total Fat 25g	**39%**
Saturated Fat 10g	**49%**
Trans Fat 0g	
Cholesterol 0mg	**0%**
Sodium 30mg	**1%**
Total Carbohydrate 5g	**2%**
Dietary Fiber 1g	**6%**
Sugars 2g	
Protein 2g	
Vitamin A 0% •	Vitamin C 0%
Calcium 0% •	Iron 20%

CHOCOLATE CHIP COOKIE DOUGH

YIELD: ~4 CUPS

168g (1¼ cups, lightly packed)	Vanilla Brown Rice Protein Powder
80g (⅔ cup)	Oat Flour
45g (½ cup)	Quick Cooking Oats
85g-128g (½-¾ cup)	No-Sugar-Added Dark Chocolate Baking Chips (to taste; I used ½ cup)
¼ teaspoon	Salt
360g (1½ cups)	Unsweetened Vanilla Almond Milk
192g (¾ cup)	Roasted Almond Butter
1 tablespoon	Vanilla Extract
2 teaspoons	Natural Butter Flavor
2 teaspoons	Liquid Stevia Extract

① In a large bowl, stir together the protein powder, oat flour, oats, chocolate chips and salt.

② In an electric stand mixer bowl fitted with a beater attachment, add the almond milk, almond butter, vanilla extract, butter flavor and stevia extract. Mix on low speed.

③ Dump the dry ingredients into the stand mixer and mix until the ingredients are fully incorporated. Scrape down the sides of the bowl if necessary. Mixture should be thick and fudgy, like cookie dough. Serve immediately, or store in a tightly sealed container in the fridge for up to 5 days.

NOTES:

❶ THE BROWN RICE PROTEIN POWDER *CANNOT* BE OMITTED AS IT ACTS AS A BINDER. IT MIGHT BE POSSIBLE TO SUBSTITUTE WITH OTHER VEGAN PROTEIN POWDERS (SUCH AS HEMP, PEA OR SOY), BUT I CAN'T VOUCH FOR THOSE. WHEY, CASEIN AND EGG WHITE PROTEIN POWDER WILL NOT WORK IN PLACE OF BROWN RICE PROTEIN POWDER.

❷ THE COOKIE DOUGH THICKENS OVER TIME AND REFRIGERATION. IF YOU ARE PREPARING THIS AHEAD OF TIME, CONSIDER ADDING A FEW MORE TABLESPOONS OF ALMOND MILK.

❸ YOU CAN USE WHATEVER NUT OR SEED BUTTER YOU LIKE IN PLACE OF THE ALMOND BUTTER – PEANUT BUTTER, CASHEW BUTTER, SUNFLOWER BUTTER, TAHINI, ETC. JUST NOTE THAT THE FLAVOR WILL BE DIFFERENT.

AS A COMPARISON, THE EQUIVALENT AMOUNT OF TOLLHOUSE® COOKIE DOUGH HAS: 280 CALORIES, 13G FAT, 36G CARBS, 0G FIBER, 24G SUGAR AND 2G PROTEIN.

Nutrition Facts
Serving Size Chocolate Chip Cookie Dough, 1/4 cup (60g)

Amount Per Serving

Calories 170	Calories from Fat 80

	%Daily Value*
Total Fat 9g	14%
Saturated Fat 1.5g	8%
Trans Fat 0g	
Cholesterol 0mg	0%
Sodium 80mg	3%
Total Carbohydrate 13g	4%
Dietary Fiber 3g	14%
Sugars 4g	
Protein 12g	

Vitamin A 0%	•	Vitamin C 0%
Calcium 8%	•	Iron 10%

PEANUT BUTTER & CHOCOLATE KRISPY TREATS

KRISPY TREATS

120g (4 cups)	Crispy Brown Rice Cereal
168g (½ cup)	Pure Maple Syrup
128g (½ cup)	Natural Peanut Butter
2 teaspoons	Vanilla Extract
1 teaspoon	Liquid Stevia Extract
⅛ teaspoon	Salt
64g (2 scoops or ⅔ cup)	Vanilla Whey Protein Powder

TOPPINGS

114g (⅔ cup)	No-Sugar-Added Dark Chocolate Baking Chips, melted
32g (1 scoop or ⅓ cup)	Vanilla Whey Protein Powder
63g (3 tablespoons)	Pure Maple Syrup
32g (2 tablespoons)	Natural Peanut Butter

FOR THE KRISPY TREATS

① Line an 8x8" brownie pan with parchment paper.
② In a medium-sized bowl, add the crispy brown rice cereal.
③ In a large microwave-safe bowl, stir together the maple syrup, peanut butter, vanilla extract, stevia extract and salt. Microwave at 15-second intervals, stirring between each one, until the mixture is runny and warm.
④ Stir the protein powder into the microwaved mixture. Dump in the crispy brown rice cereal and gently fold together. It will take a few minutes to get everything incorporated.
⑤ Scoop the mixture into the prepared pan. Flatten it out and press it down to make it compact.

FOR THE TOPPINGS

⑥ Spread the melted chocolate over the krispy treat layer. Place the pan in the fridge.
⑦ In a small bowl, stir together the protein powder, maple syrup and peanut butter.
⑧ Scoop the mixture into a piping bag with round tip (#804) and pipe the frosting over the chocolate layer. Place the pan in the fridge for 30 minutes, then slice into 16 squares. Serve immediately, or store in a tightly sealed container in the fridge with each treat placed on a square of parchment paper to prevent them from sticking. Keeps for ~1 week.

Nutrition Facts

Serving Size Peanut Butter & Chocolate Krispy Treats, 1 krispy treat

Amount Per Serving

Calories 170	Calories from Fat 70

	%Daily Value*
Total Fat 7g	11%
Saturated Fat 2g	9%
Trans Fat 0g	
Cholesterol 10mg	4%
Sodium 70mg	3%
Total Carbohydrate 22g	7%
Dietary Fiber 2g	7%
Sugars 10g	
Protein 8g	

Vitamin A 0%	•	Vitamin C 0%
Calcium 4%	•	Iron 6%

COCONUT KRISPY TREATS

120g (4 cups)	Crispy Brown Rice Cereal
30g (½ cup)	Reduced Fat Unsweetened Shredded Coconut
168g (½ cup)	Pure Maple Syrup
128g (½ cup)	Raw Coconut Butter
2 teaspoons	Vanilla Extract
1 teaspoon	Liquid Stevia Extract
½ teaspoon	Natural Coconut Flavor
⅛ teaspoon	Salt
64g (2 scoops or ⅔ cup)	Vanilla Whey Protein Powder
43g (¼ cup)	No-Sugar-Added Dark Chocolate Baking Chips, melted
5g (1 teaspoon)	Raw Coconut Butter, melted

① Line an 8x8" brownie pan with parchment paper.

② In a medium-sized bowl, add the crispy brown rice cereal and shredded coconut.

③ In a large microwave-safe bowl, stir together the maple syrup, coconut butter, vanilla extract, stevia extract, coconut flavor and salt. Microwave at 15-second intervals, stirring between each one, until the coconut butter is completely melted.

④ Stir the protein powder into the microwaved mixture. Dump in the crispy brown rice cereal and shredded coconut and gently fold together. It will take a few minutes to get everything incorporated.

⑤ Scoop the mixture into the prepared pan. Flatten it out and press it down to make it compact. Place the pan in the fridge for 30 minutes, then slice into 16 squares.

⑥ In a small bowl, stir together the melted chocolate and coconut butter. Drizzle over the sliced krispy treats. Place the krispy treats in the fridge for 30 minutes. Serve immediately, or store in a tightly sealed container in the fridge with each treat placed on a square of parchment paper to prevent them from sticking. Keeps for ~1 week.

Nutrition Facts

Serving Size Coconut Krispy Treats, 1 krispy treat

Amount Per Serving	
Calories 140	Calories from Fat 60
	%Daily Value*
Total Fat 6g	**10%**
Saturated Fat 5g	**27%**
Trans Fat 0g	
Cholesterol 10mg	**3%**
Sodium 70mg	**3%**
Total Carbohydrate 18g	**6%**
Dietary Fiber 2g	**8%**
Sugars 7g	
Protein 4g	
Vitamin A 0% •	Vitamin C 0%
Calcium 2% •	Iron 4%

PEANUT BUTTER POTS

A HEALTHIER VERSION OF REESE'S® ★ YIELD: **8 PEANUT BUTTER POTS**

4oz	No-Sugar-Added Milk Chocolate, melted
35g (¼ cup)	Powdered Erythritol
30g (¼ cup)	Peanut Flour
⅛ teaspoon	Salt
76g (⅓ cup)	Plain, Nonfat Greek Yogurt

① Spoon ~1 teaspoon of the melted chocolate into 8 cavities of a peanut butter cup mold (see Essential Kitchen Tools pg. 23). Rotate the tray at an angle to coat the cavity "walls" with the chocolate. Place in the freezer while you make the filling.

② In a medium-sized bowl, whisk together the erythritol, peanut flour and salt. Stir in the yogurt. Mixture should be thick, like frosting.

③ Scoop the filling into the chilled chocolate cups. Do not overfill.

④ Spoon the remaining melted chocolate over the filling. Refrigerate until firm. Serve immediately, or store in a tightly sealed container in the fridge for up to 1 week.

Nutrition Facts

Serving Size Peanut Butter Pots, 1 pot (30g)

Amount Per Serving

Calories 80	Calories from Fat 50

	%Daily Value*
Total Fat 6g	9%
Saturated Fat 3g	16%
Trans Fat 0g	
Cholesterol 0mg	1%
Sodium 45mg	2%
Total Carbohydrate 5g	2%
Dietary Fiber 5g	19%
Sugars < 1g	
Protein 4g	

Vitamin A 0%	•	Vitamin C 0%
Calcium 4%	•	Iron 4%

PEPPERMINT COINS

A HEALTHIER VERSION OF YORK® ★ **YIELD:** 14 PEPPERMINT COINS

140g (1 cup)	Powdered Erythritol
30g (2 tablespoons)	Water
42g (3 tablespoons)	Coconut Oil, soft
½ tablespoon	Peppermint Flavor
4oz	No-Sugar-Added Dark Chocolate, melted

① Line a cookie sheet with a silicone baking mat and line another cookie sheet with parchment paper.
② In a medium-sized bowl, stir together the erythritol and water, then stir in the coconut oil and peppermint flavor. Scoop the mixture onto the silicone baking mat and place another silicone baking mat on top. Very gently, use a rolling pin to spread the mixture out to ¼" thickness. Place in the freezer for 20 minutes.
③ Use a 2" circle cookie cutter and transfer the peppermint coins onto the cookie sheet with parchment paper using a thin, sharp pie server (keep rolling out the leftover peppermint filling until it is all used up). Freeze for 15 minutes.
④ Dip the peppermint coins into the melted chocolate and place back on the pan. Refrigerate until firm. Serve immediately, or store in a tightly sealed container in the fridge for up to 1 week.

Nutrition Facts

Serving Size Peppermint Coins, 1 coin (23g)

Amount Per Serving

Calories 70	Calories from Fat 60

	%Daily Value*
Total Fat 6g	**10%**
Saturated Fat 4.5g	**22%**
Trans Fat 0g	
Cholesterol 0mg	**0%**
Sodium 0mg	**0%**
Total Carbohydrate 3g	**1%**
Dietary Fiber 3g	**10%**
Sugars 0g	
Protein 0g	

Vitamin A 0%	•	Vitamin C 0%
Calcium 0%	•	Iron 4%

HOMEMADE CHEWY CARAMELS

YIELD: **32 CARAMELS**

153g (⅔ cup)	Light Coconut Milk, canned
56g (¼ cup)	Coconut Oil, liquid
¼ teaspoon	Salt
252g (¾ cup)	Pure Maple Syrup
30g (2 tablespoons)	Water
192g (1 cup)	Sucanat
96g (½ cup)	Granulated Erythritol
2 teaspoons	Vanilla Extract
32g (2 tablespoons)	Roasted Almond Butter

① Generously spray an 8x5" loaf pan with cooking spray and line one way with parchment paper.

② In a medium-sized bowl, whisk together the coconut milk, coconut oil and salt. Set aside.

③ In a 3-quart saucepan, add the maple syrup, water, sucanat and erythritol. Do not stir. Add a candy thermometer to the saucepan, then place the pan over a stove set to medium-high heat.

④ Without stirring, let the mixture come to a boil. When it reaches 250 degrees Fahrenheit (it takes me ~7 minutes), remove the pan from the heat and whisk in the set aside coconut milk/oil mixture.

⑤ Return the pan to the heat and let it come to a boil again. When it reaches 266 degrees Fahrenheit (it takes me ~10 minutes). Turn the stove off and remove from the heat.

⑥ *Very carefully*, add the vanilla extract. It will bubble up vigorously, so watch out!

⑦ Add the almond butter and whisk together. Pour the caramel into the prepared pan and let cool at room temperature for 3 hours.

⑧ Line a cookie sheet with parchment paper.

⑨ Transfer the caramel out of the pan and flip over onto the cookie sheet lined with parchment paper. Peel the parchment paper off the top of the caramel and refrigerate uncovered for 1½ hours.

⑩ Cut the caramel into 1" cubes with kitchen shears (kitchen shears work better than a knife). Wrap the caramels in parchment paper cut into 4" squares. Serve immediately, or store in a tightly sealed container in the fridge for up to 2 weeks.

Nutrition Facts

Serving Size Homemade Chewy Caramels, 2 caramels

Amount Per Serving

Calories 140	Calories from Fat 45

	%Daily Value*
Total Fat 5g	8%
Saturated Fat 4g	19%
Trans Fat 0g	
Cholesterol 0mg	0%
Sodium 40mg	2%
Total Carbohydrate 23g	8%
Dietary Fiber < 1g	3%
Sugars 22g	
Protein < 1g	

Vitamin A 0%	•	Vitamin C 0%
Calcium 0%	•	Iron 0%

I like to coat my caramels with dark chocolate and sprinkle them with flaked sea salt!

Cookies & Pastries

Oatmeal Raisin Cookies (pg. 56-57)

Peanut Butter Cookies (pg. 54-55)

Chocolate Crackers (pg. 52-53)

Chocolate Chip Cookies (pg. 48-49)

CHOCOLATE CHIP COOKIES

YIELD: **12 COOKIES**

180g (1½ cups)	Oat Flour
96g (½ cup)	Granulated Erythritol
1 teaspoon	Double-Acting Baking Powder
¼ teaspoon	Salt
112g (½ cup)	Coconut Oil, liquid
60g (¼ cup)	Unsweetened Vanilla Almond Milk, warm
2 teaspoons	Vanilla Extract
2 teaspoons	Natural Butter Flavor
1 teaspoon	Liquid Stevia Extract
85g (½ cup)	No-Sugar-Added Dark Chocolate Baking Chips

① Preheat the oven to 350 degrees Fahrenheit and line 2 cookie sheets with parchment paper.

② In a medium-sized bowl, whisk together the oat flour, erythritol, baking powder and salt.

③ In a large bowl, whisk together the coconut oil, almond milk, vanilla extract, butter flavor and stevia extract. Dump the dry ingredients over the wet ingredients and fold together with a silicone spatula.

④ Fold in the chocolate chips.

⑤ Scoop 2 heaping tablespoons of the cookie dough into your palms, roll it into a ball, then gently flatten it into a patty shape. Place the cookie dough patty onto the prepared cookie sheet. Do this with the rest of the cookie dough. Bake for 12 minutes.

⑥ Slide the parchment paper off the cookie sheets and onto wire cooling racks to cool. Serve immediately, or store in a tightly sealed container at room temperature for up to 3 days.

THESE COOKIES ARE DELICATELY CHEWY AND DELICIOUS! YOU'LL BE SURE TO LOVE 'EM ♥

Nutrition Facts

Serving Size Chocolate Chip Cookies, 1 cookie (46g)

Amount Per Serving

Calories 180   Calories from Fat 110

	%Daily Value*
Total Fat 12.5g	19%
Saturated Fat 10g	51%
Trans Fat 0g	
Cholesterol 0mg	0%
Sodium 90mg	4%
Total Carbohydrate 16g	5%
Dietary Fiber 3g	10%
Sugars 0g	
Protein 3g	

Vitamin A 0%	•	Vitamin C 0%
Calcium 4%	•	Iron 6%

SOFT CHOCOLATE COOKIES

YIELD: **12 COOKIES**

136g (1 cup)	Quinoa Flour
96g (½ cup)	Granulated Erythritol
40g (½ cup)	Unsweetened Natural Cocoa Powder
1 teaspoon	Double-Acting Baking Powder
¼ teaspoon	Salt
120g (½ cup)	Unsweetened Vanilla Almond Milk
56g (¼ cup)	Coconut Oil
46g (3 tablespoons)	Unsweetened Applesauce
1 teaspoon	Vanilla Extract
1 teaspoon	Liquid Stevia Extract

① Preheat the oven to 350 degrees Fahrenheit and line 2 cookie sheets with parchment paper.

② In a medium-sized bowl, whisk together the quinoa flour, erythritol, cocoa powder, baking powder and salt.

③ In a large, microwave-safe bowl, add the almond milk, coconut oil, applesauce, vanilla extract and stevia extract. Microwave at 15-second intervals, stirring between each one, until the coconut oil is melted. Dump the dry ingredients over the wet ingredients and fold together with a silicone spatula (it should look like a fluffy, wet brownie batter).

④ Use a medium cookie scoop to portion the dough equally onto the cookie sheets. Tap the pan on the counter a few times to help the cookies level out and spread a tiny bit. Bake for 10-11 minutes, or until the surface springs back when tapped.

⑤ Slide the parchment paper off the cookie sheets and onto wire cooling racks to cool. Serve immediately, or store in a tightly sealed container at room temperature for up to 3 days.

Nutrition Facts

Serving Size Soft Chocolate Cookies, 1 cookie

Amount Per Serving	
Calories 100	Calories from Fat 50

	%Daily Value*
Total Fat 6g	9%
Saturated Fat 4.5g	22%
Trans Fat 0g	
Cholesterol 0mg	0%
Sodium 90mg	4%
Total Carbohydrate 10g	3%
Dietary Fiber 2g	9%
Sugars < 1g	
Protein 1g	

Vitamin A 0%	•	Vitamin C 0%
Calcium 4%	•	Iron 4%

CHOCOLATE QUINOA CRACKERS

YIELD: **60 CRACKERS**

136g (1 cup)	Quinoa Flour
144g (¾ cup)	Granulated Erythritol
40g (½ cup)	Unsweetened Natural Cocoa Powder
1 teaspoon	Double-Acting Baking Powder
¼ teaspoon	Salt
80g (⅓ cup)	Unsweetened Vanilla Almond Milk, warm
42g (3 tablespoons)	Coconut Oil, liquid
1 teaspoon	Vanilla Extract

① Preheat the oven to 350 degrees Fahrenheit and line 2 cookie sheets with parchment paper.

② In a medium-sized bowl, whisk together the quinoa flour, erythritol, cocoa powder, baking powder and salt.

③ In an electric stand mixer bowl fitted with a beater attachment, add the almond milk, coconut oil and vanilla extract. Mix on low speed.

④ Add the dry ingredients to the stand mixer and mix until the ingredients are fully incorporated. Scrape down the sides of the bowl if necessary. Dough should be very thick and firm. It shouldn't be dry and crumbly, it should be able to be formed into a ball.

⑤ Roll the dough out in between 2 silicone baking mats until it is ~⅛" thick. Peel the top silicone baking mat off. Use a 1¾" circle cookie cutter and transfer the dough circles onto the prepared cookie sheets (keep rolling out the dough until it is all used up). Bake for 10 minutes.

⑥ Slide the parchment paper off the cookie sheets and onto wire cooling racks to cool completely. Serve immediately, or store in a tightly sealed container at room temperature for up to 1 week.

Nutrition Facts

Serving Size Chocolate Quinoa Crackers, 5 crackers (32g)

Amount Per Serving

Calories 90 — Calories from Fat 40

	%Daily Value*
Total Fat 4.5g	**7%**
Saturated Fat 3.5g	**17%**
Trans Fat 0g	
Cholesterol 0mg	**0%**
Sodium 90mg	**4%**
Total Carbohydrate 10g	**3%**
Dietary Fiber 2g	**8%**
Sugars 0g	
Protein 2g	

Vitamin A 0%	•	Vitamin C 0%
Calcium 4%	•	Iron 6%

PEANUT BUTTER COOKIES

180g (1½ cups)	Peanut Flour
128g (⅔ cup)	Granulated Erythritol
13g (2 tablespoons)	Ground Flaxseed
2 teaspoons	Double-Acting Baking Powder
½ teaspoon	Salt
128g (½ cup)	Natural Peanut Butter
123g (½ cup)	Unsweetened Applesauce
60g (¼ cup)	Unsweetened Vanilla Almond Milk
48g (¼ cup)	Granulated Erythritol, for coating

① Preheat the oven to 350 degrees Fahrenheit and line 2 cookie sheets with silicone baking mats.

② In a small bowl, whisk together the peanut flour, 128g (⅔ cup) of erythritol, flaxseed, baking powder and salt.

③ In a large bowl, whisk together the peanut butter, applesauce and almond milk. Dump the dry ingredients over the wet ingredients and fold together with a silicone spatula.

④ Scoop 2 heaping tablespoons of the cookie dough into your palms, roll it into a ball, then gently flatten it into a patty shape (these cookies don't spread much, so form them into your desired shape and thickness). Place the cookie dough patty onto the prepared cookie sheet. Do this with the rest of the cookie dough.

⑤ In a small bowl, add the 48g (¼ cup) of erythritol for the coating. Toss the cookie dough patties in to coat, then place them back on the cookie sheet. Bake for 16 minutes. Let cool *on the pan*. Serve immediately, or store in a tightly sealed container at room temperature for up to 3 days.

Nutrition Facts

Serving Size Peanut Butter Cookies, 1 cookie

Amount Per Serving

Calories 100	Calories from Fat 50

	%Daily Value*
Total Fat 6g	9%
Saturated Fat 1g	4%
Trans Fat 0g	
Cholesterol 0mg	0%
Sodium 130mg	5%
Total Carbohydrate 5g	2%
Dietary Fiber 2g	9%
Sugars 2g	
Protein 8g	

Vitamin A 0%	•	Vitamin C 0%
Calcium 6%	•	Iron 4%

OATMEAL RAISIN COOKIES

YIELD: **17 COOKIES**

144g (1 ½ cups)	Old Fashioned Rolled Oats
48g (¼ cup)	Sucanat
40g (⅓ cup)	Oat Flour
21g (3 tablespoons)	Ground Flaxseed
1 teaspoon	Ground Cinnamon
½ teaspoon	Double-Acting Baking Powder
½ teaspoon	Baking Soda
¼ teaspoon	Salt
192g (¾ cup)	Roasted Almond Butter*
120g (½ cup)	Unsweetened Vanilla Almond Milk
2 teaspoons	Vanilla Extract
1 teaspoon	Natural Butter Flavor
1 teaspoon	Liquid Stevia Extract (increase to 1 ½ teaspoons if you want super sweet cookies)
100g (¾ cup)	Raisins

① Preheat the oven to 350 degrees Fahrenheit and line 2 cookie sheets with parchment paper.

② In a small bowl, stir together the oats, sucanat, oat flour, flaxseed, cinnamon, baking powder, baking soda and salt.

③ In a large bowl, whisk together the almond butter, almond milk, vanilla extract, butter flavor and stevia extract. Dump the dry ingredients over the wet ingredients and fold together with a silicone spatula.

④ Fold in the raisins.

⑤ Scoop 2 heaping tablespoons of the cookie dough into your palms, roll it into a ball, then gently flatten it into a patty shape (these cookies don't spread much, so form them into your desired shape and thickness). Place the cookie dough patty onto the prepared cookie sheet. Do this with the rest of the cookie dough. Bake for 11-12 minutes.

⑥ Slide the parchment paper off the cookie sheets and onto wire cooling racks to cool. Serve immediately or store in a tightly sealed container at room temperature for up to 3 days.

*MY ALMOND BUTTER IS PARTICULARLY FIRM AND DRY, NOT DRIPPY. IF YOUR ALMOND BUTTER IS DRIPPY, CONSIDER REDUCING THE ALMOND MILK TO ⅓ CUP, OR, SPOON THE ALMOND BUTTER OUT FROM THE BOTTOM OF THE JAR, WHICH IS MOST OFTEN THE DRIEST PORTION BEFORE MIXING IT ALL TOGETHER.

Nutrition Facts

Serving Size Oatmeal Raisin Cookies, 1 cookie

Amount Per Serving

Calories 150		Calories from Fat 60
		%Daily Value*
Total Fat 7g		**10%**
Saturated Fat 1g		**4%**
Trans Fat 0g		
Cholesterol 0mg		**0%**
Sodium 90mg		**4%**
Total Carbohydrate 18g		**6%**
Dietary Fiber 3g		**12%**
Sugars 8g		
Protein 5g		
Vitamin A 0%	•	Vitamin C 0%
Calcium 6%	•	Iron 6%

WHITE CHOCOLATE MACADAMIA COOKIES

YIELD: **16 COOKIES**

80g (½ cup)	Brown Rice Flour
64g (⅓ cup)	Granulated Erythritol
60g (½ cup)	Oat Flour
¼ teaspoon	Salt
192g (¾ cup)	Macadamia Butter*
60g (¼ cup)	Unsweetened Vanilla Almond Milk
1 teaspoon	Vanilla Extract
1 teaspoon	Natural Butter Flavor
1 teaspoon	Liquid Stevia Extract
112g (4oz)	Homemade White Chocolate, chopped (pg. 32-33)

① Preheat the oven to 350 degrees Fahrenheit and line 2 cookie sheets with parchment paper.
② In a medium-sized bowl, whisk together the brown rice flour, erythritol, oat flour and salt.
③ In a large bowl, stir together the macadamia butter, almond milk, vanilla extract, butter flavor and stevia extract. Dump the dry ingredients over the wet ingredients and fold together with a silicone spatula.
④ Fold in the white chocolate chunks.
⑤ Use a medium cookie scoop to portion the dough equally onto the cookie sheets. Roll the cookie dough scoops into balls, then gently flatten them into patty shapes (these cookies don't spread much, so form them into your desired shape and thickness). Bake for 12-13 minutes, or until the edges are golden brown.
⑥ Slide the parchment paper off the cookie sheets and onto wire cooling racks to cool. Serve immediately or store in a tightly sealed container at room temperature for up to 3 days.

Nutrition Facts

Serving Size White Chocolate Macadamia Cookies, 1 cookie (35g)

Amount Per Serving

Calories 160	Calories from Fat 120

	%Daily Value*
Total Fat 13g	**20%**
Saturated Fat 3g	**14%**
Trans Fat 0g	
Cholesterol 0mg	**0%**
Sodium 45mg	**2%**
Total Carbohydrate 9g	**3%**
Dietary Fiber 2g	**7%**
Sugars < 1g	
Protein 2g	

Vitamin A 0%	•	Vitamin C 0%
Calcium 6%	•	Iron 6%

*SEE PG. 32 TO LEARN HOW TO MAKE YOUR OWN MACADAMIA BUTTER!

SOFT GINGERSNAPS

150g (1¼ cups)	Oat Flour
96g (½ cup)	Granulated Erythritol
68g (½ cup)	Quinoa Flour
34g (¼ cup)	Sweet White Sorghum Flour
2 teaspoons	Double-Acting Baking Powder
1½ teaspoons	Ground Cinnamon
1½ teaspoons	Ground Ginger
¼ teaspoon	Salt
120g (½ cup)	Unsweetened Vanilla Almond Milk
75g (⅓ cup)	Coconut Oil
42g (2 tablespoons)	Molasses
2 teaspoons	Vanilla Extract
2 teaspoons	Liquid Stevia Extract
1 teaspoon	Natural Butter Flavor
64g (⅓ cup)	Granulated Erythritol, for coating

① Preheat the oven to 350 degrees Fahrenheit and line 2 cookie sheets with parchment paper.

② In a medium-sized bowl, whisk together the oat flour, 96g (½ cup) of erythritol, quinoa flour, sorghum flour, baking powder, cinnamon, ginger and salt.

③ In a large, microwave-safe bowl, add the almond milk, coconut oil, molasses, vanilla extract, stevia extract and butter flavor. Microwave at 15-second intervals, stirring between each one, until the coconut oil is melted. Dump the dry ingredients over the wet ingredients and fold together with a silicone spatula (it should look like a brownie batter).

④ Refrigerate the mixture for 20 minutes.

⑤ Briefly fold the cookie dough together one last time. Use a medium cookie scoop to portion the dough equally onto the prepared cookie sheets. Roll the cookie dough scoops into balls, then gently flatten them into patty shapes (these cookies don't spread much, so form them into your desired shape and thickness). Place the cookie dough patties back onto the cookie sheets.

⑥ In a small bowl, add the 64g (⅓ cup) of erythritol for the coating. Toss the cookie dough patties in to coat, then place them back on the cookie sheet. Bake for 9-10 minutes. Let cool *on the pan*. Serve immediately or store in a tightly sealed container at room temperature for up to 3 days.

Nutrition Facts
Serving Size Soft Gingersnaps, 1 cookie

Amount Per Serving	
Calories 100	Calories from Fat 45
	%Daily Value*
Total Fat 5g	**8%**
Saturated Fat 4g	**20%**
Trans Fat 0g	
Cholesterol 0mg	**0%**
Sodium 85mg	**4%**
Total Carbohydrate 12g	**4%**
Dietary Fiber 1g	**6%**
Sugars 1g	
Protein 2g	

Vitamin A 0%	•	Vitamin C 0%
Calcium 6%	•	Iron 6%

GRAHAM CRACKERS

YIELD: **70 CRACKERS**

136g (1 cup)	Quinoa Flour
96g (½ cup)	Sucanat
80g (⅔ cup)	Oat Flour
1½ teaspoons	Ground Cinnamon
1 teaspoon	Double-Acting Baking Powder
¼ teaspoon	Salt
63g (3 tablespoons)	Pure Maple Syrup
60g (¼ cup)	Unsweetened Vanilla Almond Milk, room temperature
42g (3 tablespoons)	Coconut Oil, liquid
1 teaspoon	Vanilla Extract

① Preheat the oven to 350 degrees Fahrenheit and line 2 cookie sheets with parchment paper.

② In a large bowl, whisk together the quinoa flour, sucanat, oat flour, cinnamon, baking powder and salt.

③ In an electric stand mixer bowl fitted with a beater attachment, add the maple syrup, almond milk, coconut oil and vanilla extract. Mix on low speed.

④ Add the dry ingredients to the stand mixer and mix until the ingredients are fully incorporated. Scrape down the sides of the bowl if necessary. Mixture should be thick, like cookie dough.

⑤ Roll the dough out in between 2 silicone baking mats until it is ~⅛" thick. Peel the top silicone baking mat off. Place the rolled out dough in the refrigerator for 30 minutes.

⑥ Use a 1¾" circle cookie cutter and transfer the dough circles onto the prepared cookie sheets using a thin, sharp pie server (keep rolling out the dough until it is all used up. If it gets too soft or sticky, place it back in the refrigerator for a bit). Bake for 10 minutes, or until the edges are golden brown.

⑦ Slide the parchment paper off the cookie sheets and onto wire cooling racks to cool completely. Serve immediately, or store in a tightly sealed container at room temperature for up to 1 week.

Nutrition Facts

Serving Size Graham Crackers, 5 crackers (26g)

Amount Per Serving

Calories 130	Calories from Fat 35

	%Daily Value*
Total Fat 4g	6%
Saturated Fat 3g	14%
Trans Fat 0g	
Cholesterol 0mg	0%
Sodium 75mg	3%
Total Carbohydrate 20g	7%
Dietary Fiber 1g	6%
Sugars 10g	
Protein 2g	

Vitamin A 0%	•	Vitamin C 0%
Calcium 4%	•	Iron 4%

FRENCH MACARONS

210g   Evaporated Cane Juice, powdered in a high-speed blender (measure *after* grinding)
120g   Almond Meal, sifted through a fine mesh sieve to remove any chunks (measure *after* sifting)
100g   Organic Egg Whites (fresh, not cartoned)
¼ teaspoon   Salt
50g   Evaporated Cane Juice (see Note ❶ on pg. 66)
½ teaspoon   Vanilla Extract

① Line 3 cookie sheets with silicone baking mats or parchment paper. Prepare a piping bag with round tip (#804).
② In a small bowl, add the powdered evaporated cane juice and sifted almond meal. Set aside.
③ In an electric stand mixer bowl fitted with a whisk attachment, add the egg whites and salt. Turn the stand mixer on high speed and start a timer.
④ Slowly sprinkle in the 50g of evaporated cane juice. Whip this mixture for 6 minutes. Mixture should form stiff peaks.
⑤ Add the vanilla extract and whip for 1 more minute. Mixture should look like this →

Nutrition Facts

Serving Size French Macarons, 2 macarons/4 shells (does not include filling)

Amount Per Serving	
Calories 120	Calories from Fat 35
	%Daily Value*
Total Fat 4g	6%
Saturated Fat 0g	1%
Trans Fat 0g	
Cholesterol 0mg	0%
Sodium 50mg	2%
Total Carbohydrate 19g	6%
Dietary Fiber < 1g	3%
Sugars 18g	
Protein 3g	
Vitamin A 0% • Vitamin C 0%	
Calcium 0% • Iron 0%	

⑥ Dump the set aside evaporated cane juice/almond meal mixture into the stand mixer and fold *by hand* with a silicone spatula until fully incorporated. Do not under mix and do not over mix. Mixture should be in between "plopping" off the spatula and "flowing" like a thick ribbon.

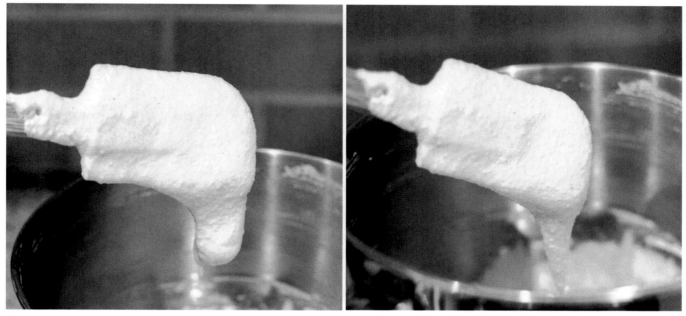

⑦ Scoop the batter into the prepared piping bag and pipe 1" buttons onto the prepared cookie sheets, each about 2" apart.
⑧ Tap the pans on the counter HARD a few times to deflate any air pockets.

⑨ Preheat the oven to 350 degrees Fahrenheit. Let the piped macarons sit at room temperature for ~1 hour. Shells should form on the surface of the macarons (when you can tap the surface, they shouldn't stick to your finger at all). Bake one tray at a time for ~8-10 minutes, or until the fluffy "feet" form and the surfaces of the macarons turn a very light golden brown. Let cool completely on the cookie sheets.

⑩ Pipe your frosting of choice (see the Frostings & Toppings section, pg. 150-159) onto half of the macaron shells, then sandwich the remaining shells on top. Serve immediately.

NOTES:

❶ DO NOT REPLACE THE POWDERED EVAPORATED CANE JUICE WITH ANY OTHER SWEETENER! YOU *CAN* REPLACE THE 50G OF GRANULATED EVAPORATED CANE JUICE WITH SUCANAT. JUST NOTE THAT THEY TAKE A LONGER TIME TO DRY BEFORE BAKING (~30 MINUTES MORE), AND THE RESULTING COLOR WILL BE A DARK TAN.

❷ USE AN OVEN THERMOMETER TO ENSURE YOUR OVEN IS EXACTLY 350 DEGREES FAHRENHEIT.

❸ USE A KITCHEN SCALE TO MAKE THIS RECIPE. IT IS *VEEEEERY* FINICKY!

❹ DO NOT USE DARK COLORED PANS TO BAKE THE MACARONS ON. USE A LIGHT COLORED PAN.

❺ DO NOT ATTEMPT THIS RECIPE ON A HUMID OR RAINY DAY.

French Macarons made with:
210g Powdered Evaporated Cane Juice
+ 50g Granulated Evaporated Cane Juice

French Macarons made with:
210g Powdered Evaporated Cane Juice
+ 50g Sucanat

Both French Macarons are photographed with
Cream Cheese Frosting (pg. 152-153) as filling

COCONUT MACAROONS

YIELD: **23 MACAROONS**

5	Large Organic Egg Whites
144g (¾ cup)	Granulated Erythritol
1 teaspoon	Vanilla Extract
1 teaspoon	Liquid Stevia Extract
¼ teaspoon	Salt
120g (2 cups)	Reduced Fat Unsweetened Shredded Coconut

① Preheat the oven to 350 degrees Fahrenheit and line a cookie sheet with parchment paper.

② In an electric stand mixer bowl fitted with a whisk attachment, add the egg whites, erythritol, vanilla extract, stevia extract and salt. Turn the stand mixer on medium speed and whip for 3 minutes. Mixture should be frothy.

③ Increase the mixer speed to high and whip for 2 minutes. Mixture should triple in volume.

④ Add the shredded coconut to the stand mixer and fold *by hand* with a silicone spatula until fully incorporated.

⑤ Use a medium cookie scoop to portion the mixture equally onto the cookie sheet. Bake for 20 minutes, or until the bottoms of the macaroons turn golden brown. Let cool on the pan. Serve immediately.

Nutrition Facts

Serving Size Coconut Macaroons, 2 macaroons

Amount Per Serving

Calories 60	Calories from Fat 40

	%Daily Value*
Total Fat 4g	**6%**
Saturated Fat 3.5g	**17%**
Trans Fat 0g	
Cholesterol 0mg	**0%**
Sodium 80mg	**3%**
Total Carbohydrate 3g	**1%**
Dietary Fiber 1g	**6%**
Sugars 0g	
Protein 2g	

Vitamin A 0%	•	Vitamin C 0%
Calcium 0%	•	Iron 0%

SWEET AFFAIR TARTS

A HEALTHIER VERSION OF POP-TARTS® ★ **YIELD: 9 TARTS**

DOUGH

200g (1⅔ cups)	Oat Flour
160g (1 cup)	Brown Rice Flour
13g (2 tablespoons)	Ground Flaxseed
½ teaspoon	Salt
123g (½ cup)	Unsweetened Applesauce
112g (½ cup)	Coconut Oil, liquid
1 teaspoon	Vanilla Extract
1 teaspoon	Natural Butter Flavor
½ teaspoon	Liquid Stevia Extract

FILLING

½ cup	100% Fruit Spread (I used Strawberry)

TOPPINGS

70g (½ cup)	Powdered Erythritol
15g (1 tablespoon)	Unsweetened Vanilla Almond Milk
2 tablespoons	DIY Rainbow Sprinkles (pg. 158-159)

FOR THE DOUGH

① Line 2 cookies sheets with parchment paper.
② In a medium-sized bowl, whisk together the oat flour, brown rice flour, flaxseed and salt.
③ In an electric stand mixer bowl fitted with a beater attachment, add the applesauce, coconut oil, vanilla extract, butter flavor and stevia extract. Mix on low speed.
④ Dump the dry ingredients into the stand mixer and mix until the ingredients are fully incorporated.
⑤ Preheat the oven to 350 degrees Fahrenheit.
⑥ Roll the dough out in between 2 silicone baking mats until it is ~⅛" thick. Slice the dough into 3x4" rectangles and transfer onto the prepared cookie sheets using a thin, sharp pie server.

FOR THE FILLING

⑦ Spread the fruit spread onto half of the dough rectangles, leaving a ½" border on all sides.
⑧ Place the remaining dough rectangles on top of the fruit spread-covered ones. With your fingertips, gently press on the outer edges of the dough to seal the tarts.

Nutrition Facts

Serving Size Sweet Affair Tarts, 1 tart

Amount Per Serving

Calories 320	Calories from Fat 130

%Daily Value*

Total Fat 14.5g	**22%**
Saturated Fat 12g	**59%**
Trans Fat 0g	
Cholesterol 0mg	**0%**
Sodium 135mg	**6%**
Total Carbohydrate 42g	**14%**
Dietary Fiber 4g	**15%**
Sugars 11g	
Protein 6g	
Vitamin A 0% •	Vitamin C 2%
Calcium 0% •	Iron 8%

⑨ With a toothpick, poke holes into the surface of the tart dough (about every inch or so). Bake for 12 minutes.
⑩ Slide the parchment paper off the cookie sheets and onto wire cooling racks to cool completely.

FOR THE TOPPINGS

⑪ In a small bowl, stir together the erythritol and almond milk.
⑫ Scoop the mixture into a piping bag with small round tip (#4) and pipe the icing over the tarts. Serve immediately, or store in a tightly sealed container at room temperature for up to 3 days.

Bars
&
Brownies

Lemon Bars (pg. 82-83)

Nanaimo Bars (pg. 80-81)

Magic Cookie Bars (pg. 78-79)

BLONDIES

YIELD: 9 BLONDIES

one 15.5oz can	Garbanzo Beans* (unseasoned)
128g (½ cup)	Roasted Almond Butter
123g (½ cup)	Unsweetened Applesauce
1 tablespoon	Vanilla Extract
1 teaspoon	Natural Butter Flavor
½ teaspoon	Liquid Stevia Extract
144g (¾ cup)	Granulated Erythritol
91g (⅔ cup)	Sweet White Sorghum Flour
½ teaspoon	Double-Acting Baking Powder
¼ teaspoon	Salt

① Preheat the oven to 350 degrees Fahrenheit and line an 8x8" brownie pan with parchment paper.

② Drain the can of garbanzo beans and pour the beans into a sieve. *Rinse well* and drain off the excess water.

③ In a food processor, add the garbanzo beans, almond butter, applesauce, vanilla extract, butter flavor and stevia extract. Purée until smooth.

④ In a medium-sized bowl, whisk together the erythritol, sorghum flour, baking powder and salt.

⑤ Dump the dry ingredients into the food processor and blend together. Scrape down the sides of the food processor and blend one more time.

⑥ Scoop the mixture into the prepared pan and spread it out. Tap the pan on the counter a few times to level out the batter. Bake for 43 minutes, or until the edges have browned slightly.

⑦ Flip the blondies onto a clean surface and peel off the parchment paper. Let the blondies cool in that position. Slice into 9 squares. Serve immediately, or store in a tightly sealed container at room temperature for up to 3 days.

SOME DELICIOUS RECIPE ADDITIONOS INCLUDE CHOCOLATE CHIPS, CHOPPED WALNUTS OR PECANS, AND EVEN DICED HOMEMADE CHEWY CARAMELS (PG. 44-45)!

*THE CAN OF GARBANZO BEANS SHOULD YIELD 1½ CUPS (240G) BEANS AFTER DRAINING AND RINSING.

Nutrition Facts

Serving Size Blondies, 1 blondie (80g)

Amount Per Serving

Calories 160	Calories from Fat 70

	%Daily Value*
Total Fat 8g	12%
Saturated Fat 0.5g	3%
Trans Fat 0g	
Cholesterol 0mg	0%
Sodium 90mg	4%
Total Carbohydrate 18g	6%
Dietary Fiber 3g	12%
Sugars 2g	
Protein 6g	

Vitamin A 0%	•	Vitamin C 2%
Calcium 6%	•	Iron 6%

I like to drizzle warm almond butter
over my blondies – absolute perfection!

FUDGE BROWNIES

YIELD: **9 BROWNIES**

one 15.5oz can	Black Beans* (unseasoned)
1 cup	Organic Blueberries (fresh not frozen)
80g (⅓ cup)	Unsweetened Vanilla Almond Milk
2 teaspoons	Vanilla Extract
½ teaspoon	Liquid Stevia Extract
96g (½ cup)	Granulated Erythritol
60g (¾ cup)	Unsweetened Natural Cocoa Powder
34g (¼ cup)	Quinoa Flour
21g (3 tablespoons)	Ground Flaxseed
1½ teaspoons	Double-Acting Baking Powder
½ teaspoon	Baking Soda
½ teaspoon	Instant Coffee Granules (optional)
¼ teaspoon	Salt
85g (½ cup)	No-Sugar-Added Dark Chocolate Baking Chips

① Preheat the oven to 350 degrees Fahrenheit and line an 8x8" brownie pan with parchment paper.

② Drain the can of black beans and pour the beans into a sieve. *Rinse well* and drain off the excess water.

③ In a food processor, add the black beans, blueberries, almond milk, vanilla extract and stevia extract. Purée until smooth.

④ In a large bowl, whisk together the erythritol, cocoa powder, quinoa flour, flaxseed, baking powder, baking soda, optional instant coffee and salt.

⑤ Pour the blended mixture (scrape out as much as you can!) into the bowl with the dry ingredients and fold together with a silicone spatula.

⑥ Fold in the chocolate chips.

⑦ Scoop the mixture into the prepared pan and spread it out. Bake for 45 minutes. Let cool completely *in the pan*.

⑧ Flip the brownies onto a clean surface and peel off the parchment paper. Slice into 9 squares. Serve immediately, or store in a tightly sealed container in the fridge for up to 3 days.

> *THE CAN OF BLACK BEANS SHOULD YIELD 1¾ CUPS (290G) BEANS AFTER DRAINING AND RINSING.

> **PEANUT BUTTER SWIRL VARIATION:**
> AFTER SCOOPING THE BATTER INTO THE PAN (STEP ⑦), SPOON ½ CUP OF WARMED NATURAL PEANUT BUTTER OVER THE BROWNIE BATTER IN 3 LINES. MAKE SWIRLS BY DRAGGING A BUTTER KNIFE THROUGH THE PEANUT BUTTER LINES. PROCEED WITH THE REST OF STEP ⑦.

Nutrition Facts

Serving Size Fudge Brownies, 1 brownie (80g)

Amount Per Serving

Calories 110	Calories from Fat 40

	%Daily Value*
Total Fat 4.5g	**7%**
Saturated Fat 2g	**10%**
Trans Fat 0g	
Cholesterol 0mg	**0%**
Sodium 240mg	**10%**
Total Carbohydrate 20g	**7%**
Dietary Fiber 7g	**28%**
Sugars 2g	
Protein 4g	

Vitamin A 0%	•	Vitamin C 2%
Calcium 15%	•	Iron 15%

MAGIC COOKIE BARS

YIELD: **16 BARS**

GRAHAM CRACKER BASE

270g (2 cups)	Graham Cracker Crumbs (I used my Graham Crackers, pg. 62-63)
¼ teaspoon	Salt
3	Large Organic Egg Whites (or ¼ cup Coconut Oil, liquid)
1 teaspoon	Natural Butter Flavor

THE LAYERS

240g (1 cup)	Unsweetened Vanilla Almond Milk
60g (1 cup)	Reduced Fat Unsweetened Shredded Coconut
1 teaspoon	Liquid Stevia Extract
56g (½ cup)	Pecans, chopped
56g (2oz)	No-Sugar-Added Dark Chocolate Baking Chips
56g (2oz)	Homemade White Chocolate, chopped (pg. 32-33)

FOR THE GRAHAM CRACKER BASE

① Preheat the oven to 350 degrees Fahrenheit and line an 8x8" brownie pan with parchment paper.

② In a medium-sized bowl, stir together the graham cracker crumbs and salt. Stir in the egg whites and butter flavor. Mixture should be thick and slightly sticky, like a graham cracker "dough" rather than a crumbly graham cracker crust.

③ Scoop the mixture into the prepared pan and flatten it out. Bake for 15 minutes.

FOR THE LAYERS

④ In a medium-sized bowl, stir together the almond milk, shredded coconut and stevia extract. Spread the mixture onto the base.

⑤ Sprinkle the chopped pecans, chocolate chips and chopped white chocolate over the coconut layer. Gently press the nuts and chocolate into the coconut layer. Bake for 24 minutes, or until the white chocolate chunks brown slightly along the edges of the pan. Let cool completely in the pan.

⑥ Transfer the bars out of the pan and slice into 16 bars. Serve immediately, or store in a tightly sealed container at room temperature for up to 3 days.

Nutrition Facts	
Serving Size Magic Cookie Bars, 1 bar	
Amount Per Serving	
Calories 160	Calories from Fat 90
	%Daily Value*
Total Fat 9.5g	15%
Saturated Fat 4.5g	24%
Trans Fat 0g	
Cholesterol 0mg	0%
Sodium 110mg	5%
Total Carbohydrate 16g	5%
Dietary Fiber 2g	8%
Sugars 7g	
Protein 3g	
Vitamin A 0% •	Vitamin C 0%
Calcium 6% •	Iron 6%

NANAIMO BARS

YIELD: **20 BARS**

BASE

135g (1 cup)	Graham Cracker Crumbs (I used my Graham Crackers, pg. 62-63)
128g (4 scoops or 1⅓ cups)	Chocolate Whey Protein Powder
15g (¼ cup)	Reduced Fat Unsweetened Shredded Coconut
10g (2 tablespoons)	Unsweetened Natural Cocoa Powder
¼ teaspoon	Salt
128g (½ cup)	Raw Coconut Butter, melted
120g (½ cup)	Unsweetened Vanilla Almond Milk, room temperature
1 teaspoon	Vanilla Extract
1 teaspoon	Natural Butter Flavor
1 teaspoon	Liquid Stevia Extract

FILLING

128g (½ cup)	Raw Coconut Butter, melted
60g (¼ cup)	Unsweetened Vanilla Almond Milk, room temperature
1 teaspoon	Vanilla Extract
1 teaspoon	Liquid Stevia Extract
70g (½ cup)	Powdered Erythritol
64g (2 scoops or ⅔ cup)	Vanilla Whey Protein Powder

CHOCOLATE LAYER

170g (1 cup)	No-Sugar-Added Dark Chocolate Baking Chips, melted

FOR THE BASE

① Line an 8x8" brownie pan with parchment paper.
② In a small bowl, whisk together the graham cracker crumbs, protein powder, shredded coconut, cocoa powder and salt.
③ In a large bowl, whisk together the coconut butter, almond milk, vanilla extract, butter flavor and stevia extract. Dump the dry ingredients over the wet ingredients and fold together.
④ Scoop the dough into the prepared pan and flatten it out. Place the pan in the fridge while you make the filling.

FOR THE FILLING

⑤ In a medium-sized bowl, whisk together the coconut butter, almond milk, vanilla extract and stevia extract.

Nutrition Facts	
Serving Size Nanaimo Bars, 1 bar	
Amount Per Serving	
Calories 190	Calories from Fat 100
	%Daily Value*
Total Fat 11.5g	18%
Saturated Fat 9g	45%
Trans Fat 0g	
Cholesterol 20mg	6%
Sodium 80mg	3%
Total Carbohydrate 13g	4%
Dietary Fiber 4g	15%
Sugars 4g	
Protein 9g	
Vitamin A 0% •	Vitamin C 0%
Calcium 6% •	Iron 8%

⑥ Whisk in the erythritol, then stir in the protein powder. Stir until the mixture is even. Mixture should look like frosting. Scoop the mixture over the chilled base and spread it out. Place the pan in the fridge for 45 minutes.

FOR THE CHOCOLATE LAYER

⑦ Spread the melted chocolate over the filling. Place the pan in the fridge for 20 minutes, or *just* until the chocolate hardens.

⑧ Slice into 20 bars. Serve immediately, or store in a tightly sealed container in the fridge with each bar placed on a square of parchment paper to prevent sticking for up to 5 days.

BASE

160g (1⅓ cups)	Oat Flour
96g (½ cup)	Granulated Erythritol
1 teaspoon	Double-Acting Baking Powder
½ teaspoon	Salt
112g (½ cup)	Coconut Oil, liquid
62g (¼ cup)	Unsweetened Applesauce
2 teaspoons	Natural Butter Flavor
1 teaspoon	Vanilla Extract

FILLING

4	Large Organic Egg Yolks
3	Large Organic Eggs
2 teaspoons	Liquid Stevia Extract
20g (2 tablespoons, packed)	Arrowroot Starch
1 teaspoon, packed	Organic Lemon Zest
240g (1 cup)	Lemon Juice, freshly squeezed

FOR THE BASE

① Adjust the oven rack to the bottom third of the oven, preheat the oven to 350 degrees Fahrenheit, and line an 8x8" brownie pan with foil.

② In a small bowl, whisk together the oat flour, erythritol, baking powder and salt.

③ In a large bowl, whisk together the coconut oil, applesauce, butter flavor and vanilla extract. Dump the dry ingredients over the wet ingredients and fold together with a silicone spatula.

④ Press the dough into the prepared pan and flatten it out.

FOR THE FILLING

⑤ In a large bowl, whisk together the egg yolks, eggs and stevia extract.

⑥ Add the arrowroot starch. Whisk vigorously until there are no clumps.

⑦ Whisk in the lemon zest and lemon juice. Whisk vigorously until the consistency is even throughout. Pour the mixture over the base. Bake for 15 minutes. Reduce the oven temperature to 300 degrees Fahrenheit and bake for another 15 minutes, or until the center no longer jiggles. Let cool completely *in the pan*, then refrigerate for 3 hours.

⑧ Transfer the bars out of the pan and slice into 16 bars. Arrange the lemon bars on a serving plate and serve, or cover with a cake dome and store in the fridge for up to 3 days.

Nutrition Facts
Serving Size Lemon Bars, 1 bar

Amount Per Serving

Calories 140	Calories from Fat 90

	%Daily Value*
Total Fat 10g	15%
Saturated Fat 7.5g	38%
Trans Fat 0g	
Cholesterol 90mg	31%
Sodium 115mg	5%
Total Carbohydrate 10g	3%
Dietary Fiber 1g	5%
Sugars < 1g	
Protein 4g	

Vitamin A 2%	•	Vitamin C 10%
Calcium 4%	•	Iron 4%

Cakes & Cupcakes

Matcha Green Tea Almond Cake (pg. 100-101)
with Coconut Frosting (pg. 154)

Strawberry Cake (pg. 98-99)
with Strawberry Frosting (pg. 154)

Red Velvet Cake (pg. 94-95)
with Classic Cheesecake (pg. 122-123) as filling
and White Chocolate Cream Cheese Frosting (pg. 152-153)

Carrot Cake (pg. 96-97)
with Cream Cheese Frosting (pg. 152-153)

VANILLA CAKE

YIELD: 2 8" CAKE LAYERS

224g (2 cups)	Coconut Flour
192g (1 cup)	Granulated Erythritol
1 tablespoon	Double-Acting Baking Powder
¼ teaspoon	Salt
369g (1½ cups)	Unsweetened Applesauce
300g (1¼ cups)	Unsweetened Vanilla Almond Milk
227g (1 cup)	Plain, Nonfat Greek Yogurt
6	Large Organic Eggs
5	Large Organic Egg Whites
1 tablespoon	Vanilla Paste
1 tablespoon	Liquid Stevia Extract
2 teaspoons	Natural Butter Flavor

① Preheat the oven to 350 degrees Fahrenheit. Spray 2 8" cake pans with cooking spray and line with 8" circle parchment paper liners.

② In a medium-sized bowl, whisk together the coconut flour, erythritol, baking powder and salt.

③ In an electric stand mixer bowl fitted with a beater attachment, add the applesauce, almond milk, yogurt, eggs, egg whites, vanilla paste, stevia extract and butter flavor. Mix on low speed.

④ Add the dry ingredients to the stand mixer and increase the mixer speed to medium. Mix until the ingredients are fully incorporated. Scrape down the sides of the bowl if necessary.

⑤ Pour the batter into the prepared cake pans. Tap the pans on the counter a few times to make sure the batter is level. Bake for 60 minutes, or until the surface springs back when tapped. Let cool completely *in the pan*.

⑥ Flip one cake layer onto a cake pedestal, peel off the parchment paper cake liner, and frost with your frosting of choice (see the Frostings & Toppings section, pg. 150-159). Flip the other cake layer onto a parchment paper-lined cookie sheet, peel off the parchment paper cake liner, then carefully slide it onto the frosted bottom cake layer (this is a delicate cake, so be careful!).

⑦ Frost the remainder of the cake. Slice and serve, or store in the fridge covered with a cake dome for up to 5 days.

Nutrition Facts	
Serving Size Vanilla Cake, 1/10th slice (does not include frosting)	
Amount Per Serving	
Calories 190	Calories from Fat 50
	%Daily Value*
Total Fat 6g	**9%**
Saturated Fat 3.5g	**18%**
Trans Fat 0g	
Cholesterol 125mg	**42%**
Sodium 320mg	**13%**
Total Carbohydrate 23g	**8%**
Dietary Fiber 10g	**40%**
Sugars 7g	
Protein 13g	
Vitamin A 4% • Vitamin C 6%	
Calcium 20% • Iron 4%	

Photographed with Cream Cheese Frosting (pg. 152-153)

CHOCOLATE CAKE

224g (2 cups)	Coconut Flour
192g (1 cup)	Granulated Erythritol
80g (1 cup)	Unsweetened Dutch Processed Cocoa Powder
2 teaspoons	Double-Acting Baking Powder
1 teaspoon	Baking Soda
¼ teaspoon	Salt
430g (1¾ cups)	Unsweetened Applesauce
320g (1⅓ cups)	Unsweetened Vanilla Almond Milk, room temperature
6	Large Organic Eggs, room temperature
4	Large Organic Egg Whites, room temperature
1 tablespoon	Vanilla Extract
1 tablespoon	Liquid Stevia Extract

① Preheat the oven to 350 degrees Fahrenheit. Spray 2 8" cake pans with cooking spray and line with 8" circle parchment paper liners.

② In a medium-sized bowl, whisk together the coconut flour, erythritol, cocoa powder, baking powder, baking soda and salt.

③ In an electric stand mixer bowl fitted with a beater attachment, add the applesauce, almond milk, eggs, egg whites, vanilla extract and stevia extract. Mix on low speed.

④ Add the dry ingredients to the stand mixer and increase the mixer speed to medium. Mix until the ingredients are fully incorporated. Scrape down the sides of the bowl if necessary.

⑤ Pour the batter into the prepared cake pans. Tap the pans on the counter a few times to make sure the batter is level. Bake for 50 minutes, or until the surface springs back when tapped. Let cool completely *in the pan.*

⑥ Flip one cake layer onto a cake pedestal, peel off the parchment paper cake liner, and frost with your frosting of choice (see the Frostings & Toppings section, pg. 150-159). Flip the other cake layer onto a parchment paper-lined cookie sheet, peel off the parchment paper cake liner, then carefully slide it onto the frosted bottom cake layer (this is a delicate cake, so be careful!).

⑦ Frost the remainder of the cake. Slice and serve, or store in the fridge covered with a cake dome for up to 5 days.

Nutrition Facts

Serving Size Chocolate Cake, 1/10th slice (does not include frosting)

Amount Per Serving	
Calories 190	Calories from Fat 60
	%Daily Value*
Total Fat 7g	**10%**
Saturated Fat 4.5g	**21%**
Trans Fat 0g	
Cholesterol 125mg	**42%**
Sodium 380mg	**16%**
Total Carbohydrate 24g	**8%**
Dietary Fiber 13g	**51%**
Sugars 6g	
Protein 12g	
Vitamin A 4% •	Vitamin C 8%
Calcium 15% •	Iron 10%

Photographed with Peanut Butter Frosting (pg. 155)

COCONUT CAKE

YIELD: **2 8" CAKE LAYERS**

224g (2 cups)	Coconut Flour
192g (1 cup)	Granulated Erythritol
1 tablespoon	Double-Acting Baking Powder
¼ teaspoon	Salt
369g (1½ cups)	Unsweetened Applesauce
345g (1½ cups)	Light Coconut Milk, canned
114g (½ cup)	Plain, Nonfat Greek Yogurt
6	Large Organic Eggs
1 tablespoon	Liquid Stevia Extract
1 tablespoon	Natural Coconut Flavor
2 teaspoons	Vanilla Extract

① Preheat the oven to 350 degrees Fahrenheit. Spray 2 8" cake pans with cooking spray and line with 8" circle parchment paper liners.

② In a medium-sized bowl, whisk together the coconut flour, erythritol, baking powder and salt.

③ In an electric stand mixer bowl fitted with a beater attachment, add the applesauce, coconut milk, yogurt, eggs, stevia extract, coconut flavor and vanilla extract. Mix on low speed.

④ Add the dry ingredients to the stand mixer and increase the mixer speed to medium. Mix until the ingredients are fully incorporated. Scrape down the sides of the bowl if necessary.

⑤ Pour the batter into the prepared cake pans. Tap the pans on the counter a few times to make sure the batter is level. Bake for 55 minutes, or until the surface springs back when tapped. Let cool completely *in the pan*.

⑥ Flip one cake layer onto a cake pedestal, peel off the parchment paper cake liner, and frost with your frosting of choice (see the Frostings & Toppings section, pg. 150-159). Flip the other cake layer onto a parchment paper-lined cookie sheet, peel off the parchment paper cake liner, then carefully slide it onto the frosted bottom cake layer (this is a delicate cake, so be careful!).

⑦ Frost the remainder of the cake. Slice and serve, or store in the fridge covered with a cake dome for up to 5 days.

Nutrition Facts

Serving Size Coconut Cake, 1/10th slice
(does not include frosting)

Amount Per Serving	
Calories 200	Calories from Fat 70

	%Daily Value*
Total Fat 8g	**12%**
Saturated Fat 6g	**29%**
Trans Fat 0g	
Cholesterol 125mg	**42%**
Sodium 270mg	**11%**
Total Carbohydrate 23g	**8%**
Dietary Fiber 10g	**40%**
Sugars 6g	
Protein 11g	

Vitamin A 4%	•	Vitamin C 6%
Calcium 15%	•	Iron 4%

Photographed with Coconut Frosting (pg. 154)

FUNFAIRY CAKE

A HEALTHIER VERSION OF FUNFETTI® ★ YIELD: 2 8" CAKE LAYERS

½ cup	DIY Rainbow Confetti (pg. 158-159)
4g (1 teaspoon, packed)	Arrowroot Starch
120g (1 cup)	Oat Flour
102g (¾ cup)	Sweet White Sorghum Flour
96g (½ cup)	Granulated Erythritol
40g (¼ cup, packed)	Arrowroot Starch
4 teaspoons	Double-Acting Baking Powder
¼ teaspoon	Salt
246g (1 cup)	Unsweetened Applesauce
180g (¾ cup)	Unsweetened Vanilla Almond Milk, room temperature
8	Large Organic Egg Whites, room temperature
56g (¼ cup)	Coconut Oil, liquid
1 tablespoon	Vanilla Paste
2 teaspoons	Natural Butter Flavor
2 teaspoons	Liquid Stevia Extract
¼ teaspoon	Almond Extract
1 tablespoon	White Vinegar

① Preheat the oven to 350 degrees Fahrenheit and spray 2 8" cake pans with cooking spray.

② In a small bowl, gently mix together the rainbow confetti and 4g (1 teaspoon) of arrowroot starch.

③ In medium-sized bowl, whisk together the oat flour, sorghum flour, erythritol, 40g (¼ cup) of arrowroot starch, baking powder and salt.

④ In an electric stand mixer bowl fitted with a beater attachment, add the applesauce, almond milk, egg whites, coconut oil, vanilla paste, butter flavor, stevia extract and almond extract. Mix on low speed.

⑤ Add the dry ingredients to the stand mixer and increase the mixer speed to medium. Mix until the ingredients are fully incorporated. Scrape down the sides of the bowl if necessary.

⑥ Add the vinegar to the stand mixer and mix one last time. Moving quickly, gently stir in the rainbow confetti, then pour the batter into the prepared cake pans. Bake for 32 minutes, or until the surface springs back when tapped. Flip the cakes onto wire cooling racks to cool completely.

⑦ Flip one cake layer onto a cake pedestal and frost with your frosting of choice (see the Frostings & Toppings section, pg. 150-159). Flip the other cake layer onto the frosted bottom cake layer.

⑧ Frost the remainder of the cake. Slice and serve, or store in the fridge covered with a cake dome for up to 5 days.

Nutrition Facts

Serving Size Funfairy Cake, 1/8th slice (does not include frosting)

Amount Per Serving

Calories 240	Calories from Fat 80
	%Daily Value*
Total Fat 9g	13%
Saturated Fat 6.5g	33%
Trans Fat 0g	
Cholesterol 0mg	0%
Sodium 380mg	16%
Total Carbohydrate 33g	11%
Dietary Fiber 3g	12%
Sugars 4g	
Protein 7g	
Vitamin A 0% •	Vitamin C 6%
Calcium 20% •	Iron 8%

Photographed with Cream Cheese Frosting (pg. 152-153)

RED VELVET CAKE

YIELD: **2 8" CAKE LAYERS**

ROASTED BEET PURÉE

4	Fist-Sized Beets

CAKE

120g (1 cup)	Oat Flour
120g (¾ cup)	Brown Rice Flour
144g (¾ cup)	Granulated Erythritol
30g (3 tablespoons, packed)	Arrowroot Starch
20g (¼ cup)	Unsweetened Natural Cocoa Powder
2 teaspoons	Double-Acting Baking Powder
¼ teaspoon	Salt
246g (1 cup)	Roasted Beet Purée, cooled to room temperature
6	Large Organic Egg Whites
120g (½ cup)	Unsweetened Vanilla Almond Milk
60g (¼ cup)	Natural Red Food Coloring (see Pantry Staples pg. 15)
56g (¼ cup)	Organic Raw Cacao Butter, melted
28g (2 tablespoons)	Coconut Oil, liquid
1½ tablespoons	Vanilla Paste
1 tablespoon	Natural Butter Flavor
1 tablespoon	Liquid Stevia Extract
1 tablespoon	White Vinegar

FOR THE ROASTED BEET PURÉE

① Preheat the oven to 400 degrees Fahrenheit.

② Rinse and gently scrub the beets, then individually wrap them in foil.

③ Place the beets on a jelly roll pan and bake for 1 hour, or until a fork pierces through the center of the beets with ease. Carefully unwrap the beets and let cool for 30 minutes.

④ Scrape off the beet skins (they should peel off easily) and chop into chunks. Add the beet chunks to a food processor and purée until completely smooth.

FOR THE CAKE

⑤ Preheat the oven to 350 degrees Fahrenheit and spray 2 8" cake pans with cooking spray.

⑥ In a medium-sized bowl, whisk together the oat flour, brown rice flour, erythritol, arrowroot starch, cocoa powder, baking powder and salt.

Nutrition Facts		
Serving Size Red Velvet Cake, 1/10th slice (does not include frosting)		
Amount Per Serving		
Calories 220		Calories from Fat 90
		%Daily Value*
Total Fat 10g		**15%**
Saturated Fat 6g		**30%**
Trans Fat 0g		
Cholesterol 0mg		**0%**
Sodium 200mg		**8%**
Total Carbohydrate 28g		**9%**
Dietary Fiber 3g		**14%**
Sugars 2g		
Protein 5g		
Vitamin A 0%	•	Vitamin C 0%
Calcium 10%	•	Iron 6%

⑦ In an electric stand mixer bowl fitted with a beater attachment, add the roasted beet purée, egg whites, almond milk, natural food coloring, melted cacao butter, coconut oil, vanilla paste, butter flavor and stevia extract. Mix on low speed.
⑧ Add the dry ingredients to the stand mixer and increase the mixer speed to medium. Mix until the ingredients are fully incorporated. Scrape down the sides of the bowl if necessary.
⑨ Add the vinegar to the stand mixer and mix one last time.
⑩ Pour the batter into the prepared cake pans. Bake for 25 minutes, or until the surface springs back when tapped. Flip the cakes onto wire cooling racks to cool completely.
⑪ Flip one cake layer onto a cake pedestal and frost with your frosting of choice (see the Frostings & Toppings section, pg. 150-159). Flip the other cake layer onto the frosted bottom cake layer.
⑫ Frost the remainder of the cake. Slice and serve (serve *only* on the day that you frost the cake, as the frosting will absorb some of the cake's color and turn pink!).

Photographed with Classic Cheesecake (pg. 122-123) as filling and White Chocolate Cream Cheese Frosting (pg. 152-153)

CARROT CAKE

YIELD: 2 8" CAKE LAYERS

224g (2 cups)	Coconut Flour
192g (1 cup)	Granulated Erythritol
1 tablespoon	Double-Acting Baking Powder
½ teaspoon	Baking Soda
1 tablespoon	Ground Cinnamon
¼ teaspoon	Ground Nutmeg
¼ teaspoon	Salt
308g (1¼ cups)	Unsweetened Applesauce
6	Large Organic Eggs
4	Large Organic Egg Whites
180g (¾ cup)	Unsweetened Vanilla Almond Milk
120g (½ cup)	100% Organic Orange Juice
21g (1 tablespoon)	Molasses
2 teaspoons	Vanilla Extract
2 teaspoons	Liquid Stevia Extract
160g (1½ cups)	Grated Organic Carrots

① Preheat the oven to 350 degrees Fahrenheit. Spray 2 8" cake pans with cooking spray and line with 8" circle parchment paper liners.

② In a medium-sized bowl, whisk together the coconut flour, erythritol, baking powder, baking soda, cinnamon, nutmeg and salt.

③ In an electric stand mixer bowl fitted with a beater attachment, add the applesauce, eggs, egg whites, almond milk, orange juice, molasses, vanilla extract and stevia extract. Mix on low speed.

④ Add the dry ingredients to the stand mixer and increase the mixer speed to medium. Mix until the ingredients are fully incorporated. Scrape down the sides of the bowl if necessary.

⑤ Add the grated carrots to the stand mixer and mix one last time.

⑥ Pour the batter into the prepared cake pans. Tap the pans on the counter a few times to make sure the batter is level. Bake for 58-60 minutes, or until the surface springs back when tapped. Let cool completely *in the pan*.

⑦ Flip one cake layer onto a cake pedestal, peel off the parchment paper cake liner, and frost with your frosting of choice (see the Frostings & Toppings section, pg. 150-159). Flip the other cake layer onto a parchment paper-lined cookie sheet, peel off the parchment paper cake liner, then carefully slide it onto the frosted bottom cake layer (this is a delicate cake, so be careful!).

⑧ Frost the remainder of the cake. Slice and serve, or store in the fridge covered with a cake dome for up to 5 days.

Nutrition Facts

Serving Size Carrot Cake, 1/10th slice (does not include frosting)

Amount Per Serving

Calories 190	Calories from Fat 50

	%Daily Value*
Total Fat 5.5g	9%
Saturated Fat 3.5g	18%
Trans Fat 0g	
Cholesterol 125mg	42%
Sodium 360mg	15%
Total Carbohydrate 24g	8%
Dietary Fiber 11g	43%
Sugars 7g	
Protein 11g	

Vitamin A 60%	•	Vitamin C 8%
Calcium 20%	•	Iron 4%

Photographed with Cream Cheese Frosting (pg. 152-153)

STRAWBERRY CAKE

YIELD: **2 8" CAKE LAYERS**

246g (1 cup)	Organic Strawberry Purée (see Instructions)
170g (1¼ cups)	Sweet White Sorghum Flour
144g (¾ cup)	Granulated Erythritol
60g (½ cup)	Oat Flour
40g (¼ cup, packed)	Arrowroot Starch
1 tablespoon	Double-Acting Baking Powder
¼ teaspoon	Salt
180g (¾ cup)	Unsweetened Vanilla Almond Milk
4	Large Organic Egg Whites
1	Large Organic Egg
75g (⅓ cup)	Coconut Oil, liquid
45g (3 tablespoons)	Natural Red Food Coloring (see Pantry Staples pg. 15)
2 teaspoons	Liquid Stevia Extract
2 teaspoons	Strawberry Flavor
1 teaspoon	Vanilla Extract
1 tablespoon	White Vinegar

① Rinse 1 pound of strawberries and slice the greens off. Add the strawberries to a food processor and purée until smooth. Measure 1 cup (use any excess purée in smoothies, yogurt, oatmeal, etc.)

② Preheat the oven to 350 degrees Fahrenheit and spray 2 8" cake pans with cooking spray.

③ In a medium-sized bowl, whisk together the sorghum flour, erythritol, oat flour, arrowroot starch, baking powder and salt.

④ In an electric stand mixer bowl fitted with a beater attachment, add the strawberry purée, almond milk, egg whites, egg, coconut oil, natural food coloring, stevia extract, strawberry flavor and vanilla extract. Mix on low speed.

⑤ Add the dry ingredients to the stand mixer and increase the mixer speed to medium. Mix until the ingredients are fully incorporated. Scrape down the sides of the bowl if necessary.

⑥ Add the vinegar to the stand mixer and mix one last time.

⑦ Pour the batter into the prepared cake pans. Bake for 28 minutes, or until the surface springs back when tapped. Flip the cakes onto wire cooling racks to cool completely.

⑧ Flip one cake layer onto a cake pedestal and frost with your frosting of choice (see the Frostings & Toppings section, pg. 150-159). Flip the other cake layer onto the frosted bottom cake layer.

⑨ Frost the remainder of the cake. Slice and serve, or store in the fridge covered with a cake dome for up to 5 days.

Nutrition Facts

Serving Size Strawberry Cake, 1/10th slice
(does not include frosting)

Amount Per Serving	
Calories 200	Calories from Fat 80

	%Daily Value*
Total Fat 9g	14%
Saturated Fat 7g	36%
Trans Fat 0g	
Cholesterol 20mg	7%
Sodium 240mg	10%
Total Carbohydrate 25g	8%
Dietary Fiber 3g	11%
Sugars 1g	
Protein 5g	

Vitamin A 0%	•	Vitamin C 25%
Calcium 15%	•	Iron 6%

Photographed with Strawberry Frosting (pg. 154)

MATCHA GREEN TEA ALMOND CAKE

YIELD: 2 8" CAKE LAYERS

224g (2 cups)	Coconut Flour
96g (½ cup)	Granulated Erythritol
2 tablespoons	Matcha Powder
1 tablespoon	Double-Acting Baking Powder
¼ teaspoon	Salt
369g (1½ cups)	Unsweetened Applesauce
300g (1¼ cups)	Unsweetened Vanilla Almond Milk
227g (1 cup)	Plain, Nonfat Greek Yogurt
6	Large Organic Eggs
5	Large Organic Egg Whites
1 tablespoon	Vanilla Extract
1 tablespoon	Liquid Stevia Extract
1 teaspoon	Almond Extract

① Preheat the oven to 350 degrees Fahrenheit. Spray 2 8" cake pans with cooking spray and line with 8" circle parchment paper liners.

② In a medium-sized bowl, whisk together the coconut flour, erythritol, matcha powder, baking powder and salt.

③ In an electric stand mixer bowl fitted with a beater attachment, add the applesauce, almond milk, yogurt, eggs, egg whites, vanilla extract, stevia extract and almond extract. Mix on low speed.

④ Add the dry ingredients to the stand mixer and increase the mixer speed to medium. Mix until the ingredients are fully incorporated. Scrape down the sides of the bowl if necessary.

⑤ Pour the batter into the prepared cake pans. Tap the pans on the counter a few times to make sure the batter is level. Bake for 60 minutes, or until the surface springs back when tapped. Let cool completely *in the pan*.

⑥ Flip one cake layer onto a cake pedestal, peel off the parchment paper cake liner, and frost with your frosting of choice (see the Frostings & Toppings section, pg. 150-159). Flip the other cake layer onto a parchment paper-lined cookie sheet, peel off the parchment paper cake liner, then carefully slide it onto the frosted bottom cake layer (this is a delicate cake, so be careful!).

⑦ Frost the remainder of the cake. Slice and serve, or store in the fridge covered with a cake dome for up to 5 days.

Nutrition Facts

Serving Size Matcha Green Tea Almond Cake, 1/10th slice (does not include frosting)

Amount Per Serving	
Calories 190	Calories from Fat 50
	%Daily Value*
Total Fat 6g	9%
Saturated Fat 3.5g	18%
Trans Fat 0g	
Cholesterol 125mg	42%
Sodium 320mg	13%
Total Carbohydrate 22g	7%
Dietary Fiber 10g	41%
Sugars 6g	
Protein 13g	
Vitamin A 4%	Vitamin C 6%
Calcium 20%	Iron 4%

Photographed with Coconut Frosting (pg. 154)

BANANA CUPCAKES

YIELD: **14 CUPCAKES**

120g (1 cup)	Oat Flour
96g (½ cup)	Granulated Erythritol
68g (½ cup)	Sweet White Sorghum Flour
68g (½ cup)	Quinoa Flour
4 teaspoons	Double-Acting Baking Powder
2 teaspoons	Ground Cinnamon
¼ teaspoon	Salt
320g (1⅓ cups)	Unsweetened Vanilla Almond Milk
320g (1¼ cups)	Mashed Bananas, very ripe
2 teaspoons	Vanilla Extract
1 teaspoon	Natural Butter Flavor
1 teaspoon	Liquid Stevia Extract
28g (2 tablespoons)	Coconut Oil, liquid

① Preheat the oven to 350 degrees Fahrenheit and spray 2 standard cupcake pans with cooking spray (this recipe makes 14 cupcakes, so you'll only need to spray 14 cavities).

② In a medium-sized bowl, whisk together the oat flour, erythritol, sorghum flour, quinoa flour, baking powder, cinnamon and salt.

③ In an electric stand mixer bowl fitted with a beater attachment, add the almond milk, mashed bananas, vanilla extract, butter flavor and stevia extract. Mix on low speed.

④ While mixing, pour the coconut oil into the stand mixer.

⑤ Add the dry ingredients to the stand mixer and increase the mixer speed to medium. Mix until the ingredients are fully incorporated. Scrape down the sides of the bowl if necessary.

⑥ Pour the batter into the prepared cupcake pans. Bake for 20 minutes, or until the surface springs back when tapped. Let cool slightly in the pans, then transfer the cupcakes to a wire cooling rack to cool completely.

⑦ Frost with your frosting of choice (see the Frostings & Toppings section, pg. 150-159). Serve immediately or store on a cake pedestal in the fridge covered with a cake dome for up to 3 days.

*IF YOU WANT TO USE CUPCAKE LINERS INSTEAD, USE PARCHMENT PAPER LINERS. THESE CUPCAKES MIGHT STICK TO PAPER LINERS.

Nutrition Facts

Serving Size Banana Cupcakes, 1 cupcake

Amount Per Serving

Calories 120	Calories from Fat 30

	%Daily Value*
Total Fat 3.5g	**5%**
Saturated Fat 2g	**10%**
Trans Fat 0g	
Cholesterol 0mg	**0%**
Sodium 180mg	**8%**
Total Carbohydrate 18.5g	**6%**
Dietary Fiber 2.5g	**10%**
Sugars 3g	
Protein 3g	

Vitamin A 0%	•	Vitamin C 4%
Calcium 15%	•	Iron 6%

Photographed with Peanut Butter Frosting (pg. 155)

YELLOW CUPCAKES

136g (1 cup)	Sweet White Sorghum Flour
120g (¾ cup)	Brown Rice Flour
96g (½ cup)	Granulated Erythritol
40g (¼ cup, packed)	Arrowroot Starch
2 teaspoons	Double-Acting Baking Powder
¼ teaspoon	Salt
246g (1 cup)	Unsweetened Applesauce
210g (¾ cup + 2 tablespoons)	Unsweetened Vanilla Almond Milk, room temperature
4	Large Organic Egg Whites, room temperature
1	Large Organic Egg, room temperature
28g (2 tablespoons)	Coconut Oil, liquid
1 tablespoon	Vanilla Paste
2 teaspoons	Natural Butter Flavor
2 teaspoons	Liquid Stevia Extract
½ teaspoon	Natural Yellow Food Coloring (see Pantry Staples pg. 15)
1 tablespoon	White Vinegar

① Preheat the oven to 350 degrees Fahrenheit and spray 2 standard cupcake pans with cooking spray (this recipe makes 18 cupcakes, so you'll only need to spray 18 cavities).

② In a medium-sized bowl, whisk together the sorghum flour, brown rice flour, erythritol, arrowroot starch, baking powder and salt.

③ In an electric stand mixer bowl fitted with a beater attachment, add the applesauce, almond milk, egg whites, egg, coconut oil, vanilla paste, butter flavor, stevia extract and natural food coloring. Mix on low speed.

④ Add the dry ingredients to the stand mixer and increase the mixer speed to medium. Mix until the ingredients are fully incorporated. Scrape down the sides of the bowl if necessary.

⑤ Add the vinegar to the stand mixer and mix one last time.

⑥ Pour the batter into the prepared cupcake pans. Bake for 20-23 minutes, or until the surface springs back when tapped. Let cool slightly in the pans, then transfer the cupcakes to a wire cooling rack to cool completely.

⑦ Frost with your frosting of choice (see the Frostings & Toppings section, pg. 150-159). Serve immediately or store on a cake pedestal in the fridge covered with a cake dome for up to 3 days.

*IF YOU WANT TO USE CUPCAKE LINERS INSTEAD, USE PARCHMENT PAPER LINERS. THESE CUPCAKES MIGHT STICK TO PAPER LINERS.

Nutrition Facts
Serving Size Yellow Cupcakes, 1 cupcake

Amount Per Serving	
Calories 90	Calories from Fat 20
	%Daily Value*
Total Fat 2.5g	4%
Saturated Fat 1.5g	8%
Trans Fat 0g	
Cholesterol 10mg	4%
Sodium 105mg	4%
Total Carbohydrate 16g	5%
Dietary Fiber 1g	5%
Sugars 2g	
Protein 2g	

Vitamin A 0%	•	Vitamin C 2%
Calcium 6%	•	Iron 2%

Photographed with Chocolate Frosting (pg. 155)

WACKY CHOCOLATE CUPCAKES

THEY'RE VEGAN! ★ YIELD: **9 CUPCAKES**

90g (⅔ cup)	Sweet White Sorghum Flour
64g (⅓ cup)	Granulated Erythritol
40g (⅓ cup)	Oat Flour
27g (⅓ cup)	Unsweetened Natural Cocoa Powder
20g (2 tablespoons, packed)	Arrowroot Starch
1 teaspoon	Xanthan Gum
1 teaspoon	Baking Soda
½ teaspoon	Double-Acting Baking Powder
½ teaspoon	Instant Coffee Granules (optional)
¼ teaspoon	Salt
300g (1¼ cups)	Unsweetened Vanilla Almond Milk
62g (¼ cup)	Unsweetened Applesauce
28g (2 tablespoons)	Coconut Oil, liquid
2 teaspoons	Vanilla Extract
1½ teaspoons	Liquid Stevia Extract
1 tablespoon	White Vinegar

① Preheat the oven to 350 degrees Fahrenheit and spray a standard cupcake pan with cooking spray (this recipe makes 9 cupcakes, so you'll only need to spray 9 cavities).

② In a medium-sized bowl, whisk together the sorghum flour, erythritol, oat flour, cocoa powder, arrowroot starch, xanthan gum, baking soda, baking powder, optional instant coffee and salt.

③ In an electric stand mixer bowl fitted with a beater attachment, add the almond milk, applesauce, coconut oil, vanilla extract and stevia extract. Mix on low speed.

④ Add the dry ingredients to the stand mixer and increase the mixer speed to medium. Mix until the ingredients are fully incorporated. Scrape down the sides of the bowl if necessary.

⑤ Add the vinegar to the stand mixer and mix on last time.

⑥ Scoop the batter into the prepared cupcake pan. Tap the pan on the counter a few times to make sure the batter is level. Bake for 22 minutes, or until the surface springs back when tapped. Let cool slightly in the pan, then transfer the cupcakes to a wire cooling rack to cool completely.

⑦ Frost with your frosting of choice (see the Frostings & Toppings section, pg. 150-159). Serve immediately or store on a cake pedestal in the fridge covered with a cake dome for up to 3 days.

*IF YOU WANT TO USE CUPCAKE LINERS INSTEAD, USE PARCHMENT PAPER LINERS. THESE CUPCAKES STICK TO PAPER LINERS.

Nutrition Facts

Serving Size Wacky Chocolate Cupcakes, 1 cupcake

Amount Per Serving

Calories 110	Calories from Fat 40

	%Daily Value*
Total Fat 4.5g	**7%**
Saturated Fat 3g	**15%**
Trans Fat 0g	
Cholesterol 0mg	**0%**
Sodium 250mg	**10%**
Total Carbohydrate 15g	**5%**
Dietary Fiber 3g	**12%**
Sugars < 1g	
Protein 2g	

Vitamin A 0%	•	Vitamin C 0%
Calcium 8%	•	Iron 4%

Photographed with Chocolate Frosting (pg. 155)
that was made with an extra splash of milk!

Breads & Muffins

Pumpkin Bread
(pg. 112-113)

Lemon Poppyseed Yogurt
Loaf (pg. 114-115)

Banana Bread
(pg. 110-111)

BANANA BREAD

YIELD: 1 LOAF (8 SLICES)

120g (1 cup)	Oat Flour
96g (½ cup)	Granulated Erythritol
68g (½ cup)	Sweet White Sorghum Flour
68g (½ cup)	Quinoa Flour
4 teaspoons	Double-Acting Baking Powder
1 tablespoon	Ground Cinnamon
¼ teaspoon	Salt
320g (1⅓ cups)	Unsweetened Vanilla Almond Milk, room temperature
320g (1¼ cups)	Mashed Bananas, very ripe
2	Large Organic Eggs, room temperature
2	Large Organic Egg Whites, room temperature
28g (2 tablespoons)	Coconut Oil, liquid
1 tablespoon	Vanilla Extract
2 teaspoons	Natural Butter Flavor
1½ teaspoons	Liquid Stevia Extract

① Preheat the oven to 350 degrees Fahrenheit and spray a 9x5x3" loaf pan with cooking spray.

② In a medium-sized bowl, whisk together the oat flour, erythritol, sorghum flour, quinoa flour, baking powder, cinnamon and salt.

③ In an electric stand mixer bowl fitted with a whisk attachment, add the almond milk, mashed bananas, eggs, egg whites, coconut oil, vanilla extract, butter flavor and stevia extract. Mix on low speed.

④ Add the dry ingredients to the stand mixer and increase the mixer speed to medium. Mix until the ingredients are fully incorporated. Scrape down the sides of the bowl if necessary.

⑤ Pour the batter into the prepared loaf pan. Bake for 60 minutes, or until the surface forms a light crust and springs back when tapped.

⑥ Transfer the loaf to a wire cooling rack to cool completely. Slice and serve, or store in a tightly sealed container in the fridge for up to 3 days.

Nutrition Facts

Serving Size Banana Bread, 1 slice

Amount Per Serving

Calories 230	Calories from Fat 60

%Daily Value*

Total Fat 7g	11%
Saturated Fat 4g	20%
Trans Fat 0g	
Cholesterol 55mg	18%
Sodium 350mg	15%
Total Carbohydrate 33g	11%
Dietary Fiber 5g	18%
Sugars 5g	
Protein 8g	

Vitamin A 4%	•	Vitamin C 6%
Calcium 25%	•	Iron 10%

PUMPKIN BREAD

YIELD: **1 LOAF (8 SLICES)**

136g (1 cup)	Sweet White Sorghum Flour
120g (¾ cup)	Brown Rice Flour
40g (¼ cup, packed)	Arrowroot Starch
96g (½ cup)	Granulated Erythritol
1 tablespoon	Ground Cinnamon
1 tablespoon	Double-Acting Baking Powder
½ teaspoon	Ground Ginger
¼ teaspoon	Ground Nutmeg
¼ teaspoon	Salt
246g (1 cup)	100% Pure Pumpkin Purée, canned
240g (1 cup)	Unsweetened Vanilla Almond Milk, room temperature
5	Large Organic Egg Whites, room temperature
28g (2 tablespoons)	Coconut Oil, liquid
2 teaspoons	Vanilla Extract
2 teaspoons	Liquid Stevia Extract
1 tablespoon	White Vinegar

① Preheat the oven to 350 degrees Fahrenheit and spray a 9x5x3" loaf pan with cooking spray.

② In a medium-sized bowl, whisk together the sorghum flour, brown rice flour, arrowroot starch, erythritol, cinnamon, baking powder, ginger, nutmeg and salt.

③ In an electric stand mixer bowl fitted with a beater attachment, add the pumpkin purée, almond milk, egg whites, coconut oil, vanilla extract and stevia extract. Mix on low speed.

④ Add the dry ingredients to the stand mixer and increase the mixer speed to medium. Mix until the ingredients are fully incorporated. Scrape down the sides of the bowl if necessary.

⑤ Add the vinegar to the stand mixer and mix one last time.

⑥ Pour the batter into the prepared loaf pan. Bake for 65 minutes, or until the surface springs back when tapped.

⑦ Transfer the loaf to a wire cooling rack to cool completely. Slice and serve, or store in a tightly sealed container in the fridge for up to 5 days.

Nutrition Facts	
Serving Size Pumpkin Bread, 1 slice	
Amount Per Serving	
Calories 190	Calories from Fat 40
	%Daily Value*
Total Fat 4.5g	**7%**
Saturated Fat 3.5g	**16%**
Trans Fat 0g	
Cholesterol 0mg	**0%**
Sodium 300mg	**13%**
Total Carbohydrate 33g	**11%**
Dietary Fiber 4g	**16%**
Sugars 1g	
Protein 5g	
Vitamin A 100% •	Vitamin C 2%
Calcium 20% •	Iron 8%

LEMON POPPYSEED YOGURT LOAF

YIELD: 1 LOAF (8 SLICES)

112g (1 cup)	Coconut Flour
96g (½ cup)	Granulated Erythritol
8g (1 tablespoon)	Poppyseeds
2 teaspoons	Double-Acting Baking Powder
¼ teaspoon	Salt
185g (¾ cup)	Unsweetened Applesauce
160g (⅔ cup)	Unsweetened Vanilla Almond Milk
114g (½ cup)	Plain, Nonfat Greek Yogurt
3	Jumbo Organic Eggs
3	Jumbo Organic Egg Whites
2 teaspoons	Organic Lemon Zest
2 teaspoons	Liquid Stevia Extract
1 teaspoon	Vanilla Paste
1 teaspoon	Natural Butter Flavor

① Preheat the oven to 350 degrees Fahrenheit and spray a 9x5x3" loaf pan with cooking spray.

② In a medium-sized bowl, whisk together the coconut flour, erythritol, poppyseeds, baking powder and salt.

③ In an electric stand mixer bowl fitted with a beater attachment, add the applesauce, almond milk, yogurt, eggs, egg whites, lemon zest, stevia extract, vanilla paste and butter flavor. Mix on low speed.

④ Add the dry ingredients to the stand mixer and increase the mixer speed to medium. Mix until the ingredients are fully incorporated. Scrape down the sides of the bowl if necessary.

⑤ Pour the batter into the prepared loaf pan. Tap the pan on the counter a few times to make sure the batter is level. Bake for 1 hour and 12 minutes, or until the surface springs back when tapped. Let cool completely *in the pan*. Cover the pan with plastic wrap and refrigerate for at least 2 hours.

⑥ Run a knife around the loaf so it will separate easily from the pan (this is a delicate loaf, so be careful!). Slice and serve, or store in a tightly sealed container in the fridge for up to 5 days.

Nutrition Facts	
Serving Size Lemon Poppyseed Yogurt Loaf, 1 slice	
Amount Per Serving	
Calories 140	Calories from Fat 40
	%Daily Value*
Total Fat 4.5g	7%
Saturated Fat 2.5g	11%
Trans Fat 0g	
Cholesterol 105mg	34%
Sodium 250mg	10%
Total Carbohydrate 14g	5%
Dietary Fiber 6g	26%
Sugars 4g	
Protein 10g	
Vitamin A 4% •	Vitamin C 4%
Calcium 15% •	Iron 4%

BLUEBERRY YOGURT MUFFINS

YIELD: **21 MUFFINS**

224g (2 cups)	Coconut Flour
192g (1 cup)	Granulated Erythritol
1 tablespoon	Double-Acting Baking Powder
¼ teaspoon	Salt
369g (1½ cups)	Unsweetened Applesauce
300g (1¼ cups)	Unsweetened Vanilla Almond Milk
227g (1 cup)	Plain, Nonfat Greek Yogurt
6	Large Organic Eggs
5	Large Organic Egg Whites
1 tablespoon	Vanilla Paste
1 tablespoon	Liquid Stevia Extract
2 teaspoons	Natural Butter Flavor
340g (2 cups)	Organic Blueberries (fresh not frozen)

① Preheat the oven to 350 degrees Fahrenheit and generously spray 2 standard cupcake pans with cooking spray (this recipe makes 21 muffins, so you'll only need to spray 21 cavities).

② In a medium-sized bowl, whisk together the coconut flour, erythritol, baking powder and salt.

③ In an electric stand mixer bowl fitted with a beater attachment, add the applesauce, almond milk, yogurt, eggs, egg whites, vanilla paste, stevia extract and butter flavor. Mix on low speed.

④ Add the dry ingredients to the stand mixer and increase the mixer speed to medium. Mix until the ingredients are fully incorporated. Scrape down the sides of the bowl if necessary.

⑤ Gently fold in the blueberries.

⑥ Scoop the batter into the prepared cupcake pans. Bake for 32 minutes, or until the edges are golden brown and the surface springs back when tapped. Let cool completely *in the pan*. Cover the pans with plastic wrap and refrigerate for at least 2 hours.

⑦ Run a knife around the muffins so they will separate easily from the pans (these are delicate muffins, so be careful!). Serve immediately, or store in a tightly sealed container in the fridge for up to 3 days.

*IF YOU WANT TO USE CUPCAKE LINERS INSTEAD, USE PARCHMENT PAPER LINERS. THESE CUPCAKES MIGHT STICK TO PAPER LINERS.

Nutrition Facts

Serving Size Blueberry Yogurt Muffins, 1 muffin (80g)

Amount Per Serving

Calories 100	Calories from Fat 25

	%Daily Value*
Total Fat 3g	4%
Saturated Fat 1.5g	9%
Trans Fat 0g	
Cholesterol 60mg	20%
Sodium 150mg	6%
Total Carbohydrate 13g	4%
Dietary Fiber 5g	20%
Sugars 5g	
Protein 6g	

Vitamin A 2%	•	Vitamin C 4%
Calcium 10%	•	Iron 0%

CINNAMON ROLLS

YIELD: **8 CINNAMON ROLLS**

DOUGH

224g (2 cups)	Organic Soy Flour
84g (¾ cup)	Coconut Flour
48g (¼ cup)	Granulated Erythritol
30g (3 tablespoons)	Psyllium Husk Powder
2 teaspoons	Double-Acting Baking Powder
¼ teaspoon	Salt
240g (1 cup)	Unsweetened Vanilla Almond Milk
187g (¾ cup)	Unsweetened Applesauce
11g (1 tablespoon)	Active Dry Yeast
2	Large Organic Eggs
2 teaspoons	Vanilla Extract
2 teaspoons	Natural Butter Flavor
2 teaspoons	Liquid Stevia Extract

CINNAMON-SUGAR FILLING

144g (¾ cup)	Granulated Erythritol
2 tablespoons	Ground Cinnamon
56g (¼ cup)	Coconut Oil, liquid
2 teaspoons	Natural Butter Flavor

DOUGH

① In a medium-sized bowl, whisk together the soy flour, coconut flour, erythritol, psyllium, baking powder and salt.

② In an electric stand mixer bowl fitted with a beater attachment, add the almond milk, applesauce and yeast. Let sit for 5 minutes.

③ Turn the stand mixer on low speed, then add the eggs, vanilla extract, butter flavor and stevia extract.

④ Add the dry ingredients to the stand mixer and increase the mixer speed to medium. Mix until the ingredients are fully incorporated. Scrape down the sides of the bowl. Mixture should be thick, like a dense brownie batter, not like typical bread dough.

⑤ Scrape down the beater attachment and the sides of the bowl. Cover the bowl with plastic wrap and place in a warm area for 1 hour.

Nutrition Facts

Serving Size Cinnamon Rolls, 1 cinnamon roll

Amount Per Serving	
Calories 280	Calories from Fat 140

	%Daily Value*
Total Fat 15.5g	**24%**
Saturated Fat 9g	**46%**
Trans Fat 0g	
Cholesterol 55mg	**18%**
Sodium 230mg	**10%**
Total Carbohydrate 22g	**7%**
Dietary Fiber 12g	**47%**
Sugars 5g	
Protein 14g	

Vitamin A 2%	•	Vitamin C 6%
Calcium 25%	•	Iron 25%

⑥ Preheat the oven to 350 degrees Fahrenheit. Scoop the dough onto a silicone baking mat and place another silicone baking mat on top. Roll the dough out into a large rectangle until it is ~½" thick. Peel the top silicone baking mat off.

CINNAMON-SUGAR FILLING

⑦ In a small bowl, whisk together the erythritol and cinnamon.

⑧ In another small bowl, stir together the coconut oil and butter flavor. Brush this onto the dough, leaving just a small amount left. Use the remaining mixture to grease a 9" springform pan.

⑨ Sprinkle the cinnamon-sugar mixture over the dough.

⑩ Gently roll the dough into a log. Make sure that the dough "seam" is on the bottom of the log so it doesn't unravel.

⑪ Slice the log into 8 and arrange the rolls inside the pan. Bake for 30 minutes, or until the surface springs back when tapped. Let cool slightly *in the pan*. Serve immediately, or store in a tightly sealed container in the fridge for up to 3 days.

Photographed with Cream Cheese Frosting (pg. 152-153)

Cheesecakes & Pies

Pecan Pie (pg. 136-137)

Pumpkin Pie (pg. 134-135)

Coconut Cream Pie (pg. 130-131)

CLASSIC CHEESECAKE

YIELD: 1 9" CHEESECAKE

GRAHAM CRACKER CRUST

270g (2 cups)	Graham Cracker Crumbs (I used my Graham Crackers, pg. 62-63)
¼ teaspoon	Salt
28g (2 tablespoons)	Coconut Oil, liquid
1	Large Organic Egg White, room temperature
1 teaspoon	Natural Butter Flavor

FILLING

16oz	Organic Neufchâtel Cream Cheese, room temperature
16oz (2 cups)	Plain, Nonfat Greek Yogurt, room temperature
2 tablespoons	Lemon Juice, freshly squeezed
1 teaspoon	Vanilla Extract
1 teaspoon	Liquid Stevia Extract
64g (2 scoops or ⅔ cup)	Vanilla Whey Protein Powder*

FOR THE GRAHAM CRACKER CRUST

① Preheat the oven to 350 degrees Fahrenheit and spray a 9" springform pan with cooking spray.

② In a medium-sized bowl, stir together the graham cracker crumbs and salt. Stir in the coconut oil, egg white and butter flavor.

③ Press the mixture into the prepared pan and flatten it out. Gently press the mixture up the sides of the pan. Bake for 10 minutes. Let cool completely.

FOR THE FILLING

④ Reduce the oven temperature to 325 degrees Fahrenheit.

⑤ In an electric stand mixer bowl fitted with a whisk attachment, add the cream cheese and yogurt. Turn the stand mixer on low speed, then increase to medium. Beat until smooth.

⑥ Add the lemon juice, vanilla extract and stevia extract. Beat until smooth.

⑦ Add the protein powder, then increase the mixer speed to high. Scrape down the sides of the bowl if necessary.

⑧ Scoop the filling into the crust and spread it out. Bake for 35 minutes, or until the center is just slightly jiggly. Let cool *in the pan*. Cover the pan with plastic wrap and refrigerate overnight. Slice and serve, or store in the fridge covered with plastic wrap for up to 1 week.

> *IF YOU DON'T WANT TO USE PROTEIN POWDER, YOU MAY SUBSTITUTE IT WITH:
> 2 Large Organic Eggs + *Additional* 1 teaspoon of Vanilla Extract + *Additional* ½ teaspoon of Stevia Extract

Nutrition Facts
Serving Size Classic Cheesecake, 1/10th slice

Amount Per Serving

Calories 320	Calories from Fat 150

	%Daily Value*
Total Fat 17g	26%
Saturated Fat 12g	61%
Trans Fat 0g	
Cholesterol 40mg	13%
Sodium 350mg	15%
Total Carbohydrate 26g	9%
Dietary Fiber 1g	4%
Sugars 14g	
Protein 14g	

Vitamin A 4%	•	Vitamin C 0%
Calcium 15%	•	Iron 4%

PEANUT BUTTER PIE

YIELD: 1 9" PIE

PEANUT BUTTER CRUST

270g (2¼ cups)	Peanut Flour
96g (½ cup)	Granulated Erythritol
1 teaspoon	Double-Acting Baking Powder
¼ teaspoon	Salt
240g (1 cup)	Unsweetened Vanilla Almond Milk
2 teaspoons	Natural Butter Flavor

FILLING

455g (2 cups)	Plain, Nonfat Greek Yogurt
240g (1 cup)	Unsweetened Vanilla Almond Milk
2 teaspoons	Liquid Stevia Extract (increase to 2½ teaspoons if you want a super sweet pie)
⅛ teaspoon	Salt
320g (2⅔ cups)	Peanut Flour

FOR THE PEANUT BUTTER CRUST

① Preheat the oven to 350 degrees Fahrenheit and spray a 9" springform pan with cooking spray.

② In a large bowl, whisk together the peanut flour, erythritol, baking powder and salt. Add the almond milk and butter flavor and fold together with a silicone spatula. Mixture should be thick, like cookie dough.

③ Press the mixture into the prepared pan and flatten it out. Press the mixture up the sides of the pan to form the shape of a crust. Bake for 22 minutes, or until the surface is firm when tapped. Let cool completely.

FOR THE FILLING

④ In an electric stand mixer bowl fitted with a whisk attachment, add the yogurt, almond milk, stevia extract and salt. Turn the stand mixer on low speed, then increase to medium. Beat until smooth.

⑤ Add the peanut flour. Beat until smooth. Scrape down the sides of the bowl if necessary.

⑥ Scoop the filling into the pie crust and spread it out. Cover the pan with plastic wrap and freeze for 2 hours. Slice and serve, or store in the fridge covered with plastic wrap for up to 1 week.

Nutrition Facts
Serving Size Peanut Butter Pie, 1/10th slice

Amount Per Serving

Calories 250	Calories from Fat 80
	%Daily Value*
Total Fat 8g	**13%**
Saturated Fat 1g	**5%**
Trans Fat 0g	
Cholesterol 0mg	**0%**
Sodium 180mg	**8%**
Total Carbohydrate 11g	**4%**
Dietary Fiber 8g	**32%**
Sugars 6g	
Protein 36g	
Vitamin A 0% •	Vitamin C 0%
Calcium 20% •	Iron 10%

GRASSHOPPER PIE

YIELD: **1 9" PIE**

CHOCOLATE CRACKER CRUST

260g (2 cups)	Chocolate Cracker Crumbs (I used my Chocolate Crackers, pg. 52-53)
¼ teaspoon	Salt
3	Large Organic Egg Whites (or 5 tablespoons Coconut Oil, liquid)

FILLING

120g (½ cup)	Unsweetened Vanilla Almond Milk
11g (1 tablespoon)	Unflavored Gelatin
660g (3 cups)	Organic Low Fat Cottage Cheese
340g (1½ cups)	Plain, Nonfat Greek Yogurt
15g (¼ cup, packed)	Organic Baby Spinach
2 teaspoons	Liquid Stevia Extract
1-1½ teaspoons	Mint Flavor (depends on how minty you want it – I used 1½ teaspoons)

FOR THE CHOCOLATE CRACKER CRUST

① Preheat the oven to 350 degrees Fahrenheit and spray a 9" springform pan with cooking spray.

② In a medium-sized bowl, stir together the chocolate cracker crumbs and salt. Stir in the egg whites. Mixture should be thick and slightly sticky, more like a chocolate "dough" rather than the typical crumbly cracker crust.

③ Scoop the mixture into the prepared pan and flatten it out. Press the dough up the sides of the pan. Bake for 15 minutes. Let cool completely.

FOR THE FILLING

④ In a medium-sized microwave-safe bowl, whisk together the almond milk and gelatin. Microwave at 15-second intervals, stirring between each one, until the mixture is warm and the gelatin has dissolved. Set aside.

⑤ In a high-speed blender, add the cottage cheese, yogurt, spinach, stevia extract and mint flavor. Purée until completely smooth.

⑥ Add the set aside almond milk/gelatin mixture into the blender. Purée until smooth. Mixture should be thick and creamy. Pour the mixture into the pie crust. Cover the pan with plastic wrap and refrigerate overnight. Slice and serve, or store in the fridge covered with plastic wrap for up to 5 days.

Nutrition Facts

Serving Size Grasshopper Pie, 1/10th slice

Amount Per Serving

Calories 160	Calories from Fat 50

	%Daily Value*
Total Fat 5.5g	**9%**
Saturated Fat 4g	**19%**
Trans Fat 0g	
Cholesterol 10mg	**3%**
Sodium 440mg	**18%**
Total Carbohydrate 13g	**4%**
Dietary Fiber 2g	**7%**
Sugars 4g	
Protein 15g	

Vitamin A 4%	•	Vitamin C 0%
Calcium 15%	•	Iron 6%

BANANA CREAM PIE

YIELD: 1 9" PIE

GRAHAM CRACKER CRUST

270g (2 cups)	Graham Cracker Crumbs (I used my Graham Crackers, pg. 62-63)
¼ teaspoon	Salt
3	Large Organic Egg Whites (reserve the yolks for the filling)
1 teaspoon	Natural Butter Flavor

FILLING

345g (1½ cups)	Light Coconut Milk, canned
1 teaspoon	Vanilla Extract
½ teaspoon	Liquid Stevia Extract
5	Large Organic Egg Yolks, room temperature
53g (⅓ cup, packed)	Arrowroot Starch
227g (1 cup)	Plain, Nonfat Greek Yogurt
½ teaspoon	Xanthan Gum
3	Large Bananas, ripe

FOR THE GRAHAM CRACKER CRUST

① Preheat the oven to 350 degrees Fahrenheit and spray a 9" springform pan with cooking spray.

② In a medium-sized bowl, stir together the graham cracker crumbs and salt. Stir in the egg whites and butter flavor. Mixture should be thick and slightly sticky, like a graham cracker "dough" rather than a crumbly graham cracker crust.

③ Scoop the mixture into the prepared pan and flatten it out. Gently press the dough up the sides of the pan. Bake for 12 minutes.

FOR THE FILLING

④ In a 1.5-quart saucepan, whisk together the coconut milk, vanilla extract and stevia extract. Place the saucepan over a stove set to medium heat.

⑤ In a large bowl, whisk together the egg yolks and arrowroot starch. It will form a very thick paste.

⑥ When the stovetop mixture is bubbling around the edges of the pan, turn the stove off.

⑦ While whisking the egg yolk mixture, slowly drizzle in the warm stovetop mixture *tablespoon by tablespoon*. Whisk constantly so you don't cook the eggs (that would be gross!). When the mixture becomes thinner, you can whisk in all of the remaining stovetop mixture.

⑧ Pour the mixture back into the saucepan and set the stove to medium-low heat. Whisk constantly until the mixture thickens. It will take some time, but the mixture will thicken almost

Nutrition Facts		
Serving Size Banana Cream Pie, 1/10th slice		
Amount Per Serving		
Calories 260	Calories from Fat 80	
		%Daily Value*
Total Fat 9g		**14%**
Saturated Fat 6g		**31%**
Trans Fat 0g		
Cholesterol 105mg		**35%**
Sodium 170mg		**7%**
Total Carbohydrate 37g		**12%**
Dietary Fiber 2g		**10%**
Sugars 16g		
Protein 7g		
Vitamin A 2%	•	Vitamin C 6%
Calcium 8%	•	Iron 8%

suddenly. When this happens, reduce the heat to low. Remove the pan from the heat when the mixture resembles a thick pudding. Let the mixture cool for 30 minutes. Whisk it occasionally so it doesn't form a skin.

⑨ Whisk in the yogurt.

⑩ *Whisking vigorously*, slowly "dash" in the xanthan gum. Mixture should thicken again.

⑪ Slice the bananas into coins and arrange them over the graham cracker crust.

⑫ Pour the filling mixture over the banana coins and spread it out. Cover the pan with plastic wrap and refrigerate overnight. Slice and serve, or store in the fridge covered with plastic wrap for up to 3 days.

COCONUT CREAM PIE

YIELD: 1 9" PIE

GRAHAM CRACKER CRUST

270g (2 cups)	Graham Cracker Crumbs (I used my Graham Crackers, pg. 62-63)
¼ teaspoon	Salt
3	Large Organic Egg Whites (or 5 tablespoons Coconut Oil, liquid)
1 teaspoon	Natural Butter Flavor

FILLING

one 14oz package	Organic Extra Firm Tofu, room temperature*
230g (1 cup)	Light Coconut Milk, canned
1 tablespoon	Vanilla Extract
1½ teaspoons	Liquid Stevia Extract
1 teaspoon	Natural Butter Flavor
256g (1 cup)	Raw Coconut Butter, melted
105g (¾ cup)	Powdered Erythritol

FOR THE GRAHAM CRACKER CRUST

① Preheat the oven to 350 degrees Fahrenheit and spray a 9" springform pan with cooking spray.

② In a medium-sized bowl, stir together the graham cracker crumbs and salt. Stir in the egg whites and butter flavor. Mixture should be thick and slightly sticky, like a graham cracker "dough" rather than a crumbly graham cracker crust.

③ Scoop the mixture into the prepared pan and flatten it out. Gently press the dough up the sides of the pan. Bake for 12 minutes. Let cool completely.

FOR THE FILLING

④ Drain the package of tofu. Place the tofu block in between some paper towels and gently press on it to remove the excess water. The block of tofu should weigh 365g after pressing.

⑤ In a food processor, add the tofu, coconut milk, vanilla extract, stevia extract and butter flavor. Purée until smooth.

⑥ While blending, pour the coconut butter into the food processor.

⑦ While blending, scoop in the erythritol. Blend until smooth.

⑧ Scoop the filling into the pie crust and spread it out. Cover the pan with plastic wrap and refrigerate overnight. Slice and serve, or store in the fridge covered with plastic wrap for up to 5 days.

Nutrition Facts	
Serving Size Coconut Cream Pie, 1/12th slice	
Amount Per Serving	
Calories 310	Calories from Fat 170
	%Daily Value*
Total Fat 18g	**28%**
Saturated Fat 15g	**73%**
Trans Fat 0g	
Cholesterol 0mg	**0%**
Sodium 140mg	**6%**
Total Carbohydrate 26g	**9%**
Dietary Fiber 5g	**18%**
Sugars 10g	
Protein 7g	
Vitamin A 0% •	Vitamin C 0%
Calcium 6% •	Iron 10%

CRÈME BRÛLÉE

303g (1⅓ cups) Plain, Nonfat Greek Yogurt
301g (1⅓ cups) Organic Low Fat Cottage Cheese
7 Large Organic Egg Yolks
(¾ cup + 3 tablespoons) Granulated Erythritol, divided
¾ teaspoon Vanilla Paste

e oven to 325 degrees Fahrenheit and place six 6oz ramekins on a jelly roll pan.

processor, add the yogurt, cottage cheese, egg yolks, 144g (¾ cup) of erythritol and vanilla paste. Purée until
nooth.

ixture evenly into the ramekins. Tap the pan on the counter a few times to remove any air pockets in the batter.
2 minutes, or until the edges are set and the center is still a little jiggly. Do not overbake! Let cool on the pan.
e remaining 36g (3 tablespoons) of erythritol over the ramekins. Use a kitchen blowtorch to caramelize the
rm a crispy shell. Serve immediately.

Nutrition Facts		
Serving Size Crème Brûlée, 1 serving		
Amount Per Serving		
Calories 140	Calories from Fat 60	
		%Daily Value*
Total Fat 7g		**10%**
Saturated Fat 3g		**15%**
Trans Fat 0g		
Cholesterol 255mg		**84%**
Sodium 210mg		**9%**
Total Carbohydrate 7g		**2%**
Dietary Fiber 0g		**0%**
Sugars 4g		
Protein 14g		
Vitamin A 6%	•	Vitamin C 0%
Calcium 15%	•	Iron 6%

PUMPKIN PIE

YIELD: 1 9" PIE

GRAHAM CRACKER CRUST

270g (2 cups)	Graham Cracker Crumbs (I used my Graham Crackers, pg. 62-63)
¼ teaspoon	Salt
28g (2 tablespoons)	Coconut Oil, liquid
1	Large Organic Egg White, room temperature
1 teaspoon	Natural Butter Flavor

FILLING

one 15oz can	100% Pure Pumpkin Purée
180g (¾ cup)	Unsweetened Vanilla Almond Milk
4	Large Organic Eggs
128g (⅔ cup)	Sucanat
2 teaspoons	Ground Cinnamon
¾ teaspoon	Ground Ginger
¼ teaspoon	Ground Nutmeg
¼ teaspoon	Salt

FOR THE GRAHAM CRACKER CRUST

① Adjust the oven rack to the bottom third of the oven, preheat the oven to 350 degrees Fahrenheit, and spray a 9"
springform pan with cooking spray.

② In a medium-sized bowl, stir together the graham cracker crumbs and salt. Stir in the coconut oil, egg white and butter flavor.

③ Press the mixture into the prepared pan and flatten it out. Gently press the mixture up the
sides of the pan. Bake for 10 minutes.

FOR THE FILLING

④ In an electric stand mixer bowl fitted with a whisk attachment, add the pumpkin purée, almond
milk and eggs. Turn the stand mixer on low speed, then increase to medium. Beat until smooth.

⑤ Add the sucanat, cinnamon, ginger, nutmeg and salt. Scrape down the sides of the bowl if
necessary.

⑥ Pour the filling into the pie crust. Bake for 50-55 minutes, or until set. Let cool completely
before serving. Slice and serve, or store in the fridge covered with plastic wrap for up to 5 days.

*ORGANIC CANNED PUMPKIN IS MUCH THICKER IN CONSISTENCY COMPARED TO CONVENTIONAL CANNED PUMPKIN. IN THIS PIE, I USED ORGANIC PUMPKIN. IF YOU USE CONVENTIONAL, CONSIDER REDUCING THE ALMOND MILK BY 2-3 TABLESPOONS.

Nutrition Facts
Serving Size Pumpkin Pie, 1/12th slice

Amount Per Serving	
Calories 210	Calories from Fat 70
	%Daily Value*
Total Fat 7.5g	12%
Saturated Fat 5g	27%
Trans Fat 0g	
Cholesterol 70mg	23%
Sodium 200mg	8%
Total Carbohydrate 31g	10%
Dietary Fiber 2g	9%
Sugars 20g	
Protein 4g	
Vitamin A 110% •	Vitamin C 2%
Calcium 8% •	Iron 8%

YIELD: 1 9" PIE

GRAHAM CRACKER CRUST

270g (2 cups)	Graham Cracker Crumbs (I used my Graham Crackers, pg. 62-63)
¼ teaspoon	Salt
60g (¼ cup)	Unsweetened Vanilla Almond Milk
28g (2 tablespoons)	Coconut Oil, liquid
1 teaspoon	Natural Butter Flavor

FILLING

half 14oz package	Organic Extra Firm Tofu*
168g (½ cup)	Pure Maple Syrup
60g (¼ cup)	Unsweetened Vanilla Almond Milk
21g (1 tablespoon)	Molasses
1 teaspoon	Vanilla Extract
96g (½ cup)	Sucanat
96g (½ cup)	Granulated Erythritol
30g (¼ cup)	Oat Flour
¼ teaspoon	Salt
112g (1 cup)	Pecans, chopped

FOR THE GRAHAM CRACKER CRUST

① Preheat the oven to 350 degrees Fahrenheit and spray a 9" springform pan with cooking spray.
② In a medium-sized bowl, stir together the graham cracker crumbs and salt. Stir in the almond milk, coconut oil and butter flavor.
③ Press the mixture into the prepared pan and flatten it out. Gently press the mixture up the sides of the pan. Bake for 11-12 minutes.

FOR THE FILLING

④ Drain the package of tofu and slice the block in half. Place one half of the tofu block in between some paper towels and gently press on it to remove the excess water. The halved block of tofu should weigh 185g after pressing.
⑤ In a food processor, add the pressed half block of tofu, maple syrup, almond milk, molasses and vanilla extract. Purée until smooth.
⑥ Add the sucanat, erythritol, oat flour and salt to the food processor. Blend until smooth.
⑦ Pour the mixture into a large mixing bowl and stir in the chopped pecans.

Nutrition Facts
Serving Size Pecan Pie, 1/12th slice

Amount Per Serving

Calories 290	Calories from Fat 120

	%Daily Value*
Total Fat 13g	20%
Saturated Fat 5g	27%
Trans Fat 0g	
Cholesterol 0mg	0%
Sodium 170mg	7%
Total Carbohydrate 39g	13%
Dietary Fiber 2g	9%
Sugars 25g	
Protein 5g	

Vitamin A 0%	•	Vitamin C 0%
Calcium 10%	•	Iron 10%

⑧ Pour the mixture into the pie crust (if you're feeling decorative, arrange some whole pecans on top!). Bake for 60-65 minutes, or until the filling is set (it shouldn't jiggle at all). Let cool completely. Cover the pan with plastic wrap and refrigerate for 2 hours. Slice and serve, or store in the fridge covered with plastic wrap for up to 1 week.

Serve this Pecan Pie with a scoop of Vanilla Bean Ice Cream (pg. 140-141) and you will know what heaven feels like!

Ice Cream

VANILLA

CHOCOLATE

MOCHA

STRAWBERRIES
AND CREAM

MATCHA

ICE CREAM-THAWING INSTRUCTIONS:
Place the container of ice cream...

<u>Option #1</u>: On the counter at room
temperature for ~2 hours.

<u>Option #2</u>: In the refrigerator for ~6 hours.

VANILLA BEAN ICE CREAM

YIELD: **6 CUPS (1.5 QUARTS)**

32oz (4 cups)	Plain, Nonfat Greek Yogurt
16oz (2 cups)	Organic Half and Half
2 teaspoons	Liquid Stevia Extract
1 teaspoon	Vanilla Paste
1 teaspoon	Xanthan Gum
¼ teaspoon	Salt

① In an electric stand mixer bowl fitted with a whisk attachment, add the yogurt, half and half, stevia extract and vanilla paste. Turn the stand mixer on low speed. Mix until smooth.

② In a small bowl, whisk together the xanthan gum and salt. With the stand mixer running, sprinkle in the dry ingredients. Increase the mixer speed to medium.

③ Churn the ice cream batter according to your ice cream machine's instructions. Freeze until it has the texture you prefer (for me, it takes around 3 hours). Serve, or you can scoop the ice cream into a tightly sealed container and store in the freezer.

CHOCOLATE CHIP VARIATION:
AFTER THE ICE CREAM CHURNING PROCESS, FOLD 1 CUP OF NO-SUGAR-ADDED DARK CHOCOLATE BAKING CHIPS INTO THE ICE CREAM.

COOKIES AND CREAM VARIATION:
AFTER THE ICE CREAM CHURNING PROCESS, FOLD 1½ CUPS OF CHOPPED CHOCOLATE CRACKERS (PG. 52-53) INTO THE ICE CREAM.

Nutrition Facts

Serving Size Vanilla Bean Ice Cream, 1 cup (227g)

Amount Per Serving

Calories 190   Calories from Fat 80

	%Daily Value*
Total Fat 9g	14%
Saturated Fat 5g	27%
Trans Fat 0g	
Cholesterol 25mg	9%
Sodium 190mg	8%
Total Carbohydrate 10g	3%
Dietary Fiber 0g	1%
Sugars 9g	
Protein 18g	

Vitamin A 6%	•	Vitamin C 0%
Calcium 25%	•	Iron 0%

CHOCOLATE ICE CREAM

YIELD: 6¼ CUPS

32oz (4 cups)	Plain, Nonfat Greek Yogurt
16oz (2 cups)	Organic Half and Half
1 tablespoon	Vanilla Extract
2½ teaspoons	Liquid Stevia Extract
40g (½ cup)	Unsweetened Dutch Processed Cocoa Powder
1 teaspoon	Xanthan Gum
¼ teaspoon	Salt

① In an electric stand mixer bowl fitted with a whisk attachment, add the yogurt, half and half, vanilla extract and stevia extract. Turn the stand mixer on low speed. Mix until smooth.

② In a small bowl, whisk together the cocoa powder, xanthan gum and salt. With the stand mixer running, sprinkle in the dry ingredients. Increase the mixer speed to medium.

③ Churn the ice cream batter according to your ice cream machine's instructions. Freeze until it has the texture you prefer (for me, it takes around 3 hours). Serve, or you can scoop the ice cream into a tightly sealed container and store in the freezer.

CHOCOLATE-PEANUT BUTTER VARIATION:
DURING STEP ①, ADD ½ CUP OF NATURAL PEANUT BUTTER, THEN PROCEED WITH STEP ②.

MINT CHOCOLATE CHIP VARIATION:
DURING STEP ①, ADD 1 TABLESPOON OF MINT FLAVOR (OR TO TASTE), THEN PROCEED WITH STEP ②. AFTER THE ICE CREAM CHURNING PROCESS, FOLD 1 CUP OF NO-SUGAR-ADDED DARK CHOCOLATE BAKING CHIPS INTO THE ICE CREAM.

Nutrition Facts

Serving Size Chocolate Ice Cream, 1 cup (225g)

Amount Per Serving	
Calories 200	Calories from Fat 90

	%Daily Value*
Total Fat 10g	15%
Saturated Fat 6g	28%
Trans Fat 0g	
Cholesterol 25mg	9%
Sodium 190mg	8%
Total Carbohydrate 13g	4%
Dietary Fiber 3g	10%
Sugars 8g	
Protein 18g	

Vitamin A 6%	•	Vitamin C 0%
Calcium 25%	•	Iron 6%

MOCHA ICE CREAM

16oz (2 cups)	Organic Half and Half
6oz (¾ cup)	Brewed Espresso
40g (½ cup)	Unsweetened Natural Cocoa Powder
¼ teaspoon	Salt
11g (1 tablespoon)	Unflavored Gelatin
32oz (4 cups)	Plain, Nonfat Greek Yogurt
1 tablespoon	Vanilla Extract
1 tablespoon	Liquid Stevia Extract

① In a 1.5-quart saucepan, add the half and half, espresso, cocoa powder and salt. Whisk until smooth.

② Place the pan over a stove set to medium heat. Whisk occasionally until the mixture starts to steam. Reduce the heat to low.

③ While whisking, sprinkle in the gelatin. Whisk until the gelatin dissolves. Turn the stove off and remove the pan from the heat. Pour the mixture into a mixing bowl, cover with plastic wrap, and let cool to room temperature (~2 hours). Refrigerate overnight.

④ In an electric stand mixer bowl fitted with a whisk attachment, add the refrigerated mixture (it will look like jello), yogurt, vanilla extract and stevia extract. Turn the stand mixer on low speed, then increase to medium. Mix until smooth.

⑤ Churn the ice cream batter according to your ice cream machine's instructions. Freeze until it has the texture you prefer (for me, it takes around 3 hours). Serve, or you can scoop the ice cream into a tightly sealed container and store in the freezer.

HAZELNUT MOCHA VARIATION:
DURING STEP ④, ADD 1 CUP OF NUTTY VELVET SPREAD (PG. 156-157), THEN PROCEED WITH STEP ⑤.

Nutrition Facts

Serving Size Mocha Ice Cream, 1 cup (227g)

Amount Per Serving

Calories 190	Calories from Fat 80

	%Daily Value*
Total Fat 8g	13%
Saturated Fat 4.5g	23%
Trans Fat 0g	
Cholesterol 25mg	8%
Sodium 170mg	7%
Total Carbohydrate 11g	4%
Dietary Fiber 2g	9%
Sugars 7g	
Protein 17g	

Vitamin A 6%	•	Vitamin C 0%
Calcium 25%	•	Iron 2%

STRAWBERRIES & CREAM ICE CREAM

YIELD: **7½ CUPS**

360g (1½ cups)	Organic Strawberry Purée (see Instructions)
32oz (4 cups)	Plain, Nonfat Greek Yogurt
16oz (2 cups)	Organic Half and Half
1 tablespoon	Vanilla Extract
2 teaspoons	Liquid Stevia Extract
1 teaspoon	Xanthan Gum
¼ teaspoon	Salt

① Rinse ~1 pound of strawberries and slice the greens off. Add the strawberries to a food processor and purée until smooth.

② In an electric stand mixer bowl fitted with a whisk attachment, add 1½ cups of the strawberry purée (use any excess purée in smoothies, yogurt, oatmeal, etc.), yogurt, half and half, vanilla extract and stevia extract. Turn the stand mixer on low speed. Mix until smooth.

③ In a small bowl, whisk together the xanthan gum and salt. With the stand mixer running, sprinkle in the dry ingredients. Increase the mixer speed to medium.

④ Churn the ice cream batter according to your ice cream machine's instructions. Freeze until it has the texture you prefer (for me, it takes around 3 hours). Serve, or you can scoop the ice cream into a tightly sealed container and store in the freezer.

Nutrition Facts

Serving Size Strawberries and Cream Ice Cream, 1 cup (230g)

Amount Per Serving

Calories 170	Calories from Fat 60

	%Daily Value*
Total Fat 7g	11%
Saturated Fat 4.5g	23%
Trans Fat 0g	
Cholesterol 20mg	7%
Sodium 160mg	7%
Total Carbohydrate 12g	4%
Dietary Fiber 1g	4%
Sugars 9g	
Protein 15g	

Vitamin A 4%	•	Vitamin C 45%
Calcium 25%	•	Iron 0%

MATCHA GREEN TEA ALMOND ICE CREAM

YIELD: 6 CUPS (1.5 QUARTS)

32oz (4 cups)	Plain, Nonfat Greek Yogurt
16oz (2 cups)	Organic Half and Half
1 tablespoon	Vanilla Extract
2 teaspoons	Liquid Stevia Extract
½ teaspoon	Almond Extract
2 tablespoons	Matcha Powder
1 teaspoon	Xanthan Gum
¼ teaspoon	Salt

① In an electric stand mixer bowl fitted with a whisk attachment, add the yogurt, half and half, vanilla extract, stevia extract and almond extract. Turn the stand mixer on low speed. Mix until smooth.

② In a small bowl, whisk together the matcha powder, xanthan gum and salt. With the stand mixer running, sprinkle in the dry ingredients. Increase the mixer speed to medium.

③ Churn the ice cream batter according to your ice cream machine's instructions. Freeze until it has the texture you prefer (for me, it takes around 3 hours). Serve, or you can scoop the ice cream into a tightly sealed container and store in the freezer.

WHITE CHOCOLATE CHUNK VARIATION:
AFTER THE ICE CREAM CHURNING PROCESS, FOLD 1 CUP OF CHOPPED HOMEMADE WHITE CHOCOLATE (PG. 32-33), INTO THE ICE CREAM. IF NOT USING THE HOMEMADE WHITE CHOCOLATE, PLEASE USE ALL-NATURAL WHITE CHOCOLATE (SOME BRANDS USE HYDROGENATED OILS IN THEIR CHOCOLATE)!

MATCHA STRAWBERRY VARIATION:
AFTER THE ICE CREAM CHURNING PROCESS, SCOOP ⅓ OF THE ICE CREAM INTO A CONTAINER AND SPREAD ¼ CUP OF 100% FRUIT STRAWBERRY SPREAD ON TOP. SCOOP ANOTHER ⅓ OF THE ICE CREAM OVER THE LAST LAYER, AND SPREAD ON ANOTHER ¼ CUP OF THE FRUIT SPREAD. SCOOP THE LAST ⅓ OF THE ICE CREAM ON TOP OF THE FRUIT SPREAD.

Nutrition Facts

Serving Size Matcha Green Tea Almond Ice Cream, 1 cup (230g)

Amount Per Serving

Calories 200	Calories from Fat 80

	%Daily Value*
Total Fat 9g	14%
Saturated Fat 5g	27%
Trans Fat 0g	
Cholesterol 30mg	10%
Sodium 190mg	8%
Total Carbohydrate 12g	4%
Dietary Fiber < 1g	4%
Sugars 9g	
Protein 19g	

Vitamin A 6%	•	Vitamin C 0%
Calcium 25%	•	Iron 0%

Frostings & Toppings

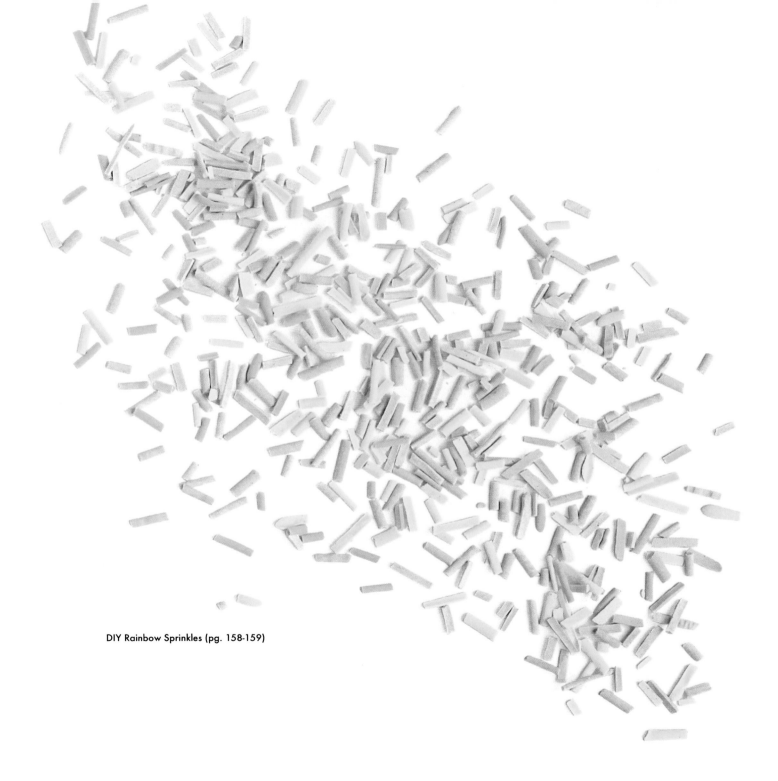

DIY Rainbow Sprinkles (pg. 158-159)

CREAM CHEESE FROSTING

YIELD: 4 CUPS

16oz	Organic Neufchâtel Cream Cheese, room temperature
12oz (1½ cups)	Plain, Nonfat Greek Yogurt
2 teaspoons	Vanilla Extract
175g (1¼ cups)	Powdered Erythritol

① In an electric stand mixer bowl fitted with a whisk attachment, add the cream cheese. Turn the stand mixer on medium speed. Beat until smooth.

② Add the yogurt, vanilla extract and erythritol. Increase the mixer speed to high and beat until smooth. Refrigerate for ~1 hour to firm up.

③ Frost!

WHITE CHOCOLATE VARIATION:
DURING STEP ①, ADD 75G (⅓ CUP) OF MELTED ORGANIC RAW CACAO BUTTER ALONG WITH THE CREAM CHEESE, THEN PROCEED WITH STEP ②.

Nutrition Facts

Serving Size Cream Cheese Frosting, 1/4 cup (60g)

Amount Per Serving

Calories 80	Calories from Fat 50
	%Daily Value*
Total Fat 5.5g	9%
Saturated Fat 3.5g	19%
Trans Fat 0g	
Cholesterol 20mg	6%
Sodium 110mg	4%
Total Carbohydrate 4g	1%
Dietary Fiber 0g	0%
Sugars 2g	
Protein 3g	
Vitamin A 0% •	Vitamin C 0%
Calcium 4% •	Iron 0%

STRAWBERRY FROSTING

YIELD: **2¾ CUPS**

16oz (2 cups)	Plain, Nonfat Greek Yogurt
2oz	Organic Neufchâtel Cream Cheese, room temperature
1 teaspoon	Liquid Stevia Extract
55g (½ cup, packed)	Freeze-Dried Organic Strawberries, ground into a powder (measure after grinding)

① In an electric stand mixer bowl fitted with a whisk attachment, add the yogurt, cream cheese and stevia extract. Turn the stand mixer on low speed, then increase to medium. Beat until smooth.
② Add the freeze-dried strawberry powder. Increase the mixer speed to high and beat until smooth. Refrigerate for ~1 hour to firm up.
③ Frost!

Nutrition Facts

Serving Size Strawberry Frosting, 1/4 cup (51g)

Amount Per Serving

Calories 50	Calories from Fat 10

	%Daily Value*
Total Fat 1g	2%
Saturated Fat 0.5g	3%
Trans Fat 0g	
Cholesterol < 5mg	1%
Sodium 35mg	1%
Total Carbohydrate 6g	2%
Dietary Fiber 1g	4%
Sugars 4g	
Protein 5g	

Vitamin A 0%	•	Vitamin C 35%
Calcium 6%	•	Iron 2%

COCONUT FROSTING

YIELD: **4 CUPS**

256g (1 cup)	Raw Coconut Butter, melted
240g (1 cup)	Unsweetened Vanilla Almond Milk, room temperature
2 teaspoons	Vanilla Extract
2 teaspoons	Liquid Stevia Extract
1 teaspoon	Natural Coconut Flavor
140g (1 cup)	Powdered Erythritol
128g (4 scoops or 1⅓ cups)	Vanilla Whey Protein Powder

① In an electric stand mixer bowl fitted with a whisk attachment, add the coconut butter, almond milk, vanilla extract, stevia extract and coconut flavor. Turn the stand mixer on low speed, then increase to medium. Beat until smooth.
② Add the erythritol, then add the protein powder. Increase the mixer speed to high and beat until smooth. Refrigerate for ~1 hour to firm up.
③ Frost!

Nutrition Facts

Serving Size Coconut Frosting, 1/4 cup (50g)

Amount Per Serving

Calories 140	Calories from Fat 80

	%Daily Value*
Total Fat 9g	14%
Saturated Fat 8g	41%
Trans Fat 0g	
Cholesterol 15mg	5%
Sodium 30mg	1%
Total Carbohydrate 6g	2%
Dietary Fiber 3g	10%
Sugars 1g	
Protein 7g	

Vitamin A 0%	•	Vitamin C 0%
Calcium 6%	•	Iron 4%

CHOCOLATE FROSTING

YIELD: **4⅓ CUPS**

Nutrition Facts
Serving Size Chocolate Frosting, 1/4 cup (64g)

Amount Per Serving

Calories 100	Calories from Fat 60
	%Daily Value*
Total Fat 6.5g	**10%**
Saturated Fat 3.5g	**18%**
Trans Fat 0g	
Cholesterol 0mg	**0%**
Sodium 10mg	**0%**
Total Carbohydrate 14g	**5%**
Dietary Fiber 3g	**12%**
Sugars 0g	
Protein 3g	
Vitamin A 0%	Vitamin C 0%
Calcium 6%	Iron 10%

one 14oz package	Organic Extra Firm Tofu, room temperature*
210g (1½ cups)	Powdered Erythritol
180g (¾ cup)	Unsweetened Vanilla Almond Milk
1 tablespoon	Natural Butter Flavor
2 teaspoons	Vanilla Extract
340g (2 cups)	No-Sugar-Added Dark Chocolate Baking Chips, melted

① Drain the package of tofu. Place the tofu block in between some paper towels and gently press on it to remove the excess water. The block of tofu should weigh 365g after pressing.
② In a food processor, add the tofu, erythritol, almond milk, butter flavor and vanilla extract. Purée until smooth.
③ While blending, pour the melted chocolate into the food processor. Refrigerate for ~1 hour to firm up.
④ Frost!

PEANUT BUTTER FROSTING

YIELD: **~2½ CUPS**

Nutrition Facts
Serving Size Peanut Butter Frosting, 1/4 cup (60g)

Amount Per Serving

Calories 70	Calories from Fat 20
	%Daily Value*
Total Fat 2g	**3%**
Saturated Fat 0g	**1%**
Trans Fat 0g	
Cholesterol 0mg	**0%**
Sodium 15mg	**1%**
Total Carbohydrate 4g	**1%**
Dietary Fiber 2g	**8%**
Sugars 2g	
Protein 10g	
Vitamin A 0%	Vitamin C 0%
Calcium 6%	Iron 4%

8oz (1 cup)	Plain, Nonfat Greek Yogurt
80g (⅓ cup)	Unsweetened Vanilla Almond Milk
150g (1¼ cups)	Peanut Flour
140g (1 cup)	Powdered Erythritol

① In an electric stand mixer bowl fitted with a whisk attachment, add the yogurt and almond milk. Turn the stand mixer on low speed, then increase to medium. Beat until smooth.
② Add the peanut flour and erythritol. Increase the mixer speed to high and beat until smooth. Refrigerate for ~1 hour to firm up.
③ Frost!

NUTTY VELVET SPREAD

A HEALTHIER VERSION OF NUTELLA® ★ **YIELD: 2½ CUPS**

256g (1 cup)	Hazelnut Butter
240g (1 cup)	Unsweetened Vanilla Almond Milk
1 teaspoon	Liquid Stevia Extract
105g (¾ cup)	Powdered Erythritol
60g (¾ cup)	Unsweetened Dutch Processed Cocoa Powder
⅛ teaspoon	Salt

FOR THE HAZELNUT BUTTER

① Add ~2 cups of hazelnuts (I used raw hazelnuts, but you can use roasted if you like) to a food processor. Pulse it a few times until the nuts turn into crumbles.

② Process for ~15 minutes straight, or until completely smooth. Scrape down the sides of the food processor when necessary (hazelnuts are probably the most difficult nut to "butterize" so it will take some time and patience. It usually takes me ~15 minutes of processing, scraping down the bowl, processing again, etc.).

FOR THE NUTTY VELVET SPREAD

③ In an electric stand mixer bowl fitted with a whisk attachment, add the hazelnut butter, almond milk and stevia extract. Turn the stand mixer on low speed. Mix until smooth.

④ In a small bowl, stir together the erythritol, cocoa powder and salt. With the stand mixer running, sprinkle in the dry ingredients. Increase the mixer speed to medium. Scrape down the sides of the bowl if necessary. Serve immediately, or store in a tightly sealed container in the fridge for ~1 week.

*FOR A MORE AUTHENTIC FLAVOR (AND IF YOU DON'T HAVE A DAIRY ALLERGY), USE ORGANIC WHOLE MILK INSTEAD OF ALMOND MILK!

Nutrition Facts

Serving Size Nutty Velvet Spread, 2 tbs (33g)

Amount Per Serving

Calories 90	Calories from Fat 80
	%Daily Value*
Total Fat 8g	**13%**
Saturated Fat 1g	**4%**
Trans Fat 0g	
Cholesterol 0mg	**0%**
Sodium 25mg	**1%**
Total Carbohydrate 3g	**1%**
Dietary Fiber 2g	**9%**
Sugars < 1g	
Protein 2g	
Vitamin A 0% •	Vitamin C 0%
Calcium 4% •	Iron 6%

DIY RAINBOW SPRINKLES & CONFETTI

YIELD: ~2 CUPS SPRINKLES & CONFETTI

175g (1¼ cups)	Powdered Erythritol
40g (¼ cup, packed)	Arrowroot Starch
¼ teaspoon	Salt
53g (3½ tablespoons)	Water
9g (1 heaping teaspoon)	Vanilla Paste
4 colors	Natural Food Coloring (see Note below for measurements)

① Place 4 sheets of parchment paper onto your countertop. Prepare a disposable piping bag with small round tip (#4). Have 3 more disposable piping bags handy for the various other colors.

② In a medium-sized bowl, stir together the erythritol, arrowroot starch and salt. Stir in the water and vanilla paste. The mixture should be like a <u>very</u> thick, dense dough.

③ Divide the mixture into 4 small bowls.

④ Stir in one food coloring per bowl. Mixtures should look like frosting, they should not be runny or liquidy.

⑤ Scoop one bowl's mixture into the prepared piping bag. Pipe half of the mixture as lines and the other half as small dots/confetti (use 2 sheets of parchment paper for the lines and the other 2 sheets for the confetti). When you run out of one color, rinse the piping tip, place it in a new disposable piping bag, and then fill the bag with the next color. Repeat this until all mixtures are used up.

⑥ Let the lines and confetti sit uncovered at room temperature for *at least* 12 hours in order for them to dry and firm up.

⑦ Carefully slice the rainbow lines with a knife, or pick them up and gently break them with your thumb and forefinger. Pour the sprinkles into a tightly sealed container (I used a 16oz mason jar).

⑧ Gently push the confetti off the parchment paper with your finger. Pour the confetti into another container (I used another mason jar). Store the sprinkles and confetti in the tightly sealed containers in the fridge for up to 2 months.

NOTE:
FOR THE PINK: I USED ~¼ TEASPOON OF NATURES FLAVORS®/SEELECT TEA® NATURAL CHERRY RED FOOD COLORING
FOR THE YELLOW: I USED ~¼ TEASPOON OF NATURES FLAVORS®/SEELECT TEA® NATURAL YELLOW FOOD COLORING
FOR THE GREEN: I USED ~¼ TEASPOON OF NATURES FLAVORS®/SEELECT TEA® NATURAL FOREST GREEN FOOD COLORING
FOR THE BLUE: I USED ~¼ TEASPOON OF NATURES FLAVORS®/SEELECT TEA® NATURAL BLUE FOOD COLORING

Nutrition Facts
Serving Size DIY Rainbow Sprinkles & Confetti, 1 tablespoon (7g)

Amount Per Serving	
Calories 5	Calories from Fat 0

	%Daily Value*
Total Fat 0g	0%
Saturated Fat 0g	0%
Trans Fat 0g	
Cholesterol 0mg	0%
Sodium 20mg	1%
Total Carbohydrate 2g	1%
Dietary Fiber 0g	0%
Sugars 0g	
Protein 0g	

Vitamin A 0%	•	Vitamin C 0%
Calcium 0%	•	Iron 0%

DIY Rainbow Confetti

DIY Rainbow Sprinkles

Banana Cupcakes (pg. 102-103) with Peanut Butter Frosting (pg. 155)

Peanut Butter Pie (pg. 124-125)

Chocolate Chip Cookies (pg. 48-49)

Cinnamon Rolls (pg. 118-119) with Cream Cheese Frosting (pg. 152-153)

Yellow Cupcakes (pg. 104-105) with Chocolate Frosting (pg. 155)

Pumpkin Pie (pg. 134-135)

Pecan Pie (pg. 136-137)